Tirana Modern

Tirana Modern

*Biblio–Ethnography on
the Margins of Europe*

MATTHEW ROSEN

VANDERBILT UNIVERSITY PRESS
Nashville, Tennessee

Library of Congress Cataloging-in-Publication Data
Names: Rosen, Matthew, 1977– author.
Title: Tirana modern : biblio-ethnography on the margins of Europe /
   Matthew Rosen.
Description: Nashville : Vanderbilt University Press, 2022. | Includes
   bibliographical references and index.
Identifiers: LCCN 2022002740 (print) | LCCN 2022002741 (ebook) | ISBN
   9780826504814 (paperback) | ISBN 9780826504821 (hardcover) | ISBN
   9780826504838 (epub) | ISBN 9780826504845 (pdf)
Subjects: LCSH: Albanians—Books and reading. | Tirana (Albania)—Social
   conditions. | Tirana (Albania)—History. | Literature and
   society—Albania. | Literature and anthropology—Albania. |
   Books—Albania—History. | Albania—Social conditions. |
   Albania—History. | Albania—Social life and customs.
Classification: LCC DR997.3 .R67 2022 (print) | LCC DR997.3 (ebook) | DDC
   028/.9094965—dc23/eng/20220210
LC record available at https://lccn.loc.gov/2022002740
LC ebook record available at https://lccn.loc.gov/2022002741

For the book readers
In Tirana and beyond

Contents

Illustrations

Acknowledgments

My first thanks go to Ataol Kaso and Arlind Novi. Every step I took in researching and writing this book depended on their openness to my curiosity and to the depth of the empirical traces they left for me to follow. For their friendship (and for sharing their table at Meti's with me) I also owe heartfelt thanks to Eligers Elezi, Orges Novi, and Joli Lemaj.

For their enduring and much appreciated hospitality, I thank the extended Musaraj and Dibra families, especially Mimoza and Vullnet Musaraj, Ervehe Musaraj, Vila Gjashta, Dita Musaraj, Nina Dibra, Toni Dibra, and Vilma Dedja. For offering kindness and other forms of help along the way, I likewise thank Penar Musaraj, Brizi Musaraj, Bersi Gjashta, Giti Dibra, Joli Dirba, Brikena Hoxha, Elvis Hoxha, Enis Sulstarova, Diana Malaj, Klodi Leka, Ylljet Aliçka, Besar Likmeta, Edi Vathi, Erzen Pashaj, Hektor Metani, Armanda Hysa, Nebi Bardhoshi, Olsi Lelaj, Shpëtim Sala, the *bukanist* I call Mihal, and the many other good and great book readers, writers, translators, publishers, and sellers I encountered in the field.

Language training for this project was supported by Arizona State University's Melikian Center Fellows Award and the Berkowitz Albanian Award. I am thankful to the donors, Mr. and Mrs. Gregory J. Melikian and Dr. Elaine H. Berkowitz, and to my teachers at the Critical Languages Institute in Tirana, Eljon Doçe and Liridona Sinishtaj Doçe.

Research in summers 2017, 2018, 2019, and 2021 was supported by grants from Ohio University's Baker Fund, the College of Arts and Sciences Humanities Research Fund, and the Ohio University Research Committee. I am grateful to all the committee members and external reviewers who saw merit in this project.

I am likewise grateful to the organizers and participants of the professional meetings where I first presented and received valuable peer feedback on the concepts and arguments I developed around biblio-ethnography, reading nearby, ordinary tragedy, and the circuit of books on Tirana's streets. In particular, I thank Giulia Battaglia, Elisabetta Costa, and Philipp Budka of the EASA Media Anthropology Network Workshop in 2021; Magda Buchczyk, Aimée Joyce, and Zahira Aragüete-Toribio of the EASA Biennial Conference in 2020; Jessica Symons, Andrew Irving, and Nigel Rapport of the RAI Conference in 2018; and Eeva Berglund, Francesca De Luca, Adolfo Estalella, Fran Martínez, Anna Lisa Ramella, Chiara Pussetti, and Tomás Sánchez Criado of the #Colleex (Collaboratory for Ethnographic Experimentation) Workshop in 2017.

Earlier versions of the third, fourth, and fifth chapters were published in modified form. "Reading Nearby" appeared first, in summer 2019, in *Anthropology and Humanism* (44, no. 1: 70–87). "Between Conflicting Systems" came next, in winter 2019, in the *Anthropological Journal of European Cultures* (28, no. 2: 1–22). "In the Public Interest" was originally prepared for the collection *Remitting, Restoring, and Building Contemporary Albania*, edited by Nataša Gregorič Bon and Smoki Musaraj (2021). It is reproduced here with permission of Palgrave Macmillan. I am grateful to Nataša, Smoki, David Syring (*Anthropology and Humanism*), and Elisabeth Timm (*AJEC*) for all of their generous and helpful editorial suggestions.

The idea for the title, *Tirana Modern*, came from a conjunction of conversations before the project officially began, with the late Carol Breckenridge in New York, and after the research was underway, with Olsi Lelaj in Tirana. At the New School for Social Research, Oz Frankel introduced me to "chapters in the history of the book," which put me on the path to biblio-ethnography. My graduate advisors Vyjayanthi Rao and Hugh Raffles were similarly influential in shaping my approach to research and writing.

At Vanderbilt University Press, I want to thank Zack Gresham, the editorial committee, everyone on the production and marketing teams, and the anonymous reviewers they enrolled. I am grateful to all for their time and constructive engagement with the manuscript.

Among the friends, mentors, and students I met at Ohio University, I owe special thanks to Briju Thankachan, Diane Ciekawy, Haley Duschinski, Nancy Tatarek, Chris Mattley, Marina Peterson, Úrsula Castellaño, Cindy Anderson, Steve Scanlon, Charlie Morgan, Jieli Li, Nicole Kaufman, Rachel Terman, Kara Tabor, Saumya Pant, Delphine de Gryse,

Nelli Gurbanova, Megan Westervelt, Christiana Botic, Rachel Broughton, Maddie Hordinski, and Luvina Cooley.

For their longstanding support and encouragement, my thanks also go to my parents, Susan and Barry Rosen, my three sisters, Catherine Beach, Elizabeth Julian, and Emily Cosgrove, and their respective families. Finally, my last and deepest thanks go to Simone Musaraj Rosen, a true inspiration, and Smoki Musaraj, my first and most important connection to Tirana.

Writing the Relationship between Books and People

The whole question is to see whether the *event* of the social can be extended all the way to the *event* of reading through the medium of the text.

—LATOUR 2005, 133

Has a book ever changed your life? Of course. But how? How does one account for the difference a book makes in a person's life? These apparently simple questions open the way for *biblio-ethnography*—a writing of the relationship between books and people. As a genre of ethnography, biblio-ethnography can describe any book-related account of social life. The book you hold in your hands is a specific example; it tells a story of Albanian modernity, written from the perspective of my participation in the social lives of a community of readers based in the capital, Tirana. But before turning to the topic of literary culture in post-communist Albania, I need to say a few more words about what biblio-ethnography is and how it contributes to anthropology as a discipline.

Biblio-ethnography offers a method for pursuing two basic questions. What do people do with books? And what do books do with people? The first question is easy enough to answer. People read, write, translate, publish, print, transport, display, buy, sell, lend, trade, arrange, store, annotate, interpret, recommend, discuss, debate, censor, smuggle, ban, and even burn books. The list of things people do with books could go on and on. But a closer look at any of these actions is sure to reveal a complex bundle of relationships that would take more than any one book to unravel. This is just the sort of puzzle biblio-ethnography was made to consider. Why do hyper-literate communities, including academic communities, tend to take books for granted? A big part of the reason has to do with the way most of us are taught, and have learned, to think about books in terms of their contents. Thus William Ivins, a pioneer in the history of the book, in what is probably his best-known work, *Prints and Visual Communication*, wrote, "A book, so far as it contains a text, is a container of exactly repeatable word symbols arranged in an exactly repeatable order" (Ivins 1953, 2).

The ease with which any reader with an internet connection can locate this quotation reinforces the point Ivins wanted to make about the five-thousand-year history of books.[1] But as an object, a form of technology, and a "means to produce the social," most any book on close inspection can be found to act, in Bruno Latour's (2005) vocabulary, not as an *intermediary* but as a *mediator*. That is to say, rather than reliably transporting meaning "without transformation," books very often "transform, translate, distort, and modify the meaning or elements they are supposed to carry" (Latour 2005, 39). When books act as mediators, they do not merely contain and communicate stories, ideas, or information. Rather, as bibliographers and librarians have long known—and book historians have shown with increasing sophistication—books themselves can be agents of change and participants in the production of endless idiosyncrasies.[2] This simple claim—that books act—is the main premise for doing biblio-ethnography. But to say books make things happen is not to say they cause or determine other actions or situations. It is rather, as my interlocutors in the field might say, that books can help people.

People like Klodi Leka, for example: "Your publishing house changed my life," Leka said to the publishers Ataol Kaso and Arlind Novi, who had established a custom of donating a copy of each new book they published to the community library of Organizata Politike, a left-wing activist organization based in Tirana, of which Leka was a member.[3] As a serious reader who only reads Albanian, Leka can be counted among the group of people who have benefited most from the work Kaso and Novi are doing. With a joking manner that nevertheless communicated an underlying truth, Leka continued, "We've sort of exploited you," he said. "We've had the good part of the deal."

It is telling how Leka moved in this exchange from acknowledging the publishing house as an agent of change to sympathizing with the challenges his friends faced as small publishers in Tirana. Reflecting exchanges like this one, my general argument is that the production, circulation, and consumption of books under diverse and changing circumstances can help to create and sustain—always through transformations and translations—new and unexpected relationships and identities that otherwise would not exist.

Because books participate in everything from constructing social relationships and creating new value systems to mediating individual experience and motivating collective action, there are perhaps as many justifications for tracing connections between books and people as there are ethnographers who have seen fit to make something of the books their informants have read, treasured, discussed, or displayed. Sacred texts such as the Talmud, the Qur'an, and the Bible, for example, have long enjoyed a place of prominence in ethnographies concerned with religious practice and the formation of ethical subjectivities. A wide range of storybooks and other pedagogical texts have similarly featured in ethnographies concerned with modern education and literacy practices. Novels stored in an elder informant's round mud house in Tanzania or read by young subway riders in Japan have likewise made their way into productive anthropological analyses. Several book-length ethnographies have even focused on fans of a particular author or genre of fiction. But considering all the ways in which books are made to act in social life, I still think—and I hope to show—that biblio-ethnography has more to contribute.[4]

A Wide-Angle View of Books as Technologies of Imagination

As observable traces of contact between readers, writers, translators, and publishers of every sort of subject matter imaginable, books participate in opening up the imaginative capacities of living communities in irreducibly indeterminate ways. Like newer sorts of things noted for their generative capacities—such as the internet (Humphrey 2009) and machine code (Leach 2009)—I count printed books among the "technologies of the imagination" that David Sneath, Martin Holbraad, and Morten Axel Pederson characterized as being "particularly good at opening up spaces" in which "undetermined outcomes" can emerge (2009, 25).

To Sneath, Holbraad, and Pederson, technologies "count" as being "of the imagination" when "they serve to precipitate outcomes that they do not fully condition" (2009, 25). Since words like "imagination" and "outcomes" are so abstract, let me elaborate here with the help of a short story, a tale from the field, told by Arlind, one of the avid readers I follow in this account. In the middle of a broader conversation about "the transformative effects of literacy and reading," Arlind related the following narrative about a childhood friend, who was sixteen or seventeen years old in 2003, when the story began. "When I read a book that I find extremely beautiful or fantastic," Arlind said, "the first thing I want to do is give it to a friend and say, 'You should read this.'"

> This is what happened when I read the stories of Karl Čapek. They were short, riveting, highly imaginative stories. In that epoch [the early 2000s], reading was a kind of—. It was like converting to a new religion. Something very special. I first gave the book of Karl Čapek stories to my brother [Orges]. After me, Orges read it. He also found it was beautiful. As I had passed it to him, he passed it to his friend. This friend was a thief. He also read the stories of Karl Čapek. One day, he was sent to prison, and he asked Orges for a copy of the book. Orges's friend, the thief, thought that book would help him escape from prison. How do I know? From the prison psychologist.[5] The thief was using literacy, using literature to escape prison. He was using the stories of Karl Čapek to seduce the prison psychologist, to help him escape. When I last met him, he was reading Nietzsche. This is the danger of literature in a country like Albania, where people are rootless, and one day they read Karl Čapek or Nietzsche. When this thief got out of prison, he started a business selling pirated books. We know many people here like Don Quixote, who read Nietzsche, or Heidegger. This is the chivalrous literature of our time. This is why I say reading should not be solitary but collective—so you don't fall into madness.[6]

It is with reference to stories like this that I consider books to be technologies of imagination. There is not room here to follow all the curious trails issuing outward from the story of the thief from Elbasan who believed a book of short stories could help him escape from prison. The point is to indicate what sorts of capacities books generate in Albanian social spaces. Arlind's story (and he has many more like it) also illustrates the importance of doing biblio-ethnography with a wide-angle lens. As Debra Spitulnik (2010) has argued for media anthropology more generally, widening the frame here means allowing more of the scene to be included in the picture of what people do and say "in relation" to various media (Couldry 2010, 41) and how those media are "incorporated into everyday communicative and cultural practices" (Bird 2010, 86). Most importantly, as Jens Kjaerulff has stressed, this emphatic turn to practice only remains worthwhile if in our empirical commitment to studying "what people actually do" (including attempting to seduce prison psychologists with the help of Karl Čapek stories) we are at the same time "prepared to be surprised and heed what we in fact find" (Kjaerulff 2010, 215).

Tirana Modern

As an ethnography about the role and meaning of literature in people's lives, *Tirana Modern* belongs to the sub-disciplinary context of a re-emergent literary anthropology, defined here generally as an approach to studying interactions between literature and social life (Rapport 2012).[7] While such interactions can take many forms and serve many purposes, the coherence of literary anthropology as an academic field is rooted in the recognition of socio-cultural anthropology as a discipline based on writing and interpretation.[8] As Ellen Wiles (2020) has pointed out, literary anthropology's first branch grew from the insight that literature made good ethnographic source material.[9] Traveling in the other direction, from anthropology to literature, a second branch of the subfield has worked to establish a more literary mode of writing ethnography.[10] Finally, the third and still least developed branch of literary anthropology has grown slowly but achieved definite results by using ethnographic methods to study socially embedded practices of reading and writing.[11]

With its focus on the real social relationships surrounding a specific circuit of books, the present biblio-ethnography is a product of this third branch. It does not, however, take reading and writing to be the "core objects" of analysis. This is because, like Mark Hobart, who recognized that the Balinese media practices he wanted to study "only partly overlap with direct engagement in the medium" (1999, 14), my ethnographic interest in books included the dispersed and everyday practices that surrounded them—from walking through and browsing the shelves of local bookstores to understanding, commenting on, and criticizing the contents of particular books.[12] Using a method I call *reading nearby*, I thus worked outward from book-related practices to the wider social lives of a literary community based in the capital city of a small country on the margins of Europe.[13]

The country, Albania, seems to attract superlative descriptions of all kinds. These have often, though not exclusively, been produced by outside observers. That it was "the first" civilization in Europe was a fiction promoted by the former Communist regime (Bon 2019, 201). That it was "the last" Balkan state to gain its independence from the Ottoman Empire is a flat historical fact (Abrahams 2015, 4). These also are facts: At the midpoint between the end of World War II and the fall of the Berlin Wall, Albania was the smallest and poorest of the European Communist nations (Keefe et al. 1971, 1). At the start of its transition to capitalism, in the early 1990s, it was "Europe's least developed country" (Zickel and Iwaskiw 1994, 57). A quarter of a century later, in 2019, it ranked as the "most corrupt" country (tied with North Macedonia) among European Union member and candidate states (Transparency International 2019).

Albania's legacies of Ottoman domination, harsh communism, and the everyday forms of violence that have accompanied its uneven transition to post-socialist late capitalism invite forms of analysis that map well onto Sherry Ortner's (2016) categories of "dark anthropology" and "anthropology of the good."[14] By dark anthropology Ortner meant an "anthropology that emphasizes the harsh and brutal dimensions of human experience, and the structural and historical conditions that produce them" (2016, 49). Ortner's anthropology of the good, by contrast, focuses on "what gives life a sense of purpose or direction, or how people search for the best way to live—even in dire and hostile circumstances" (Walker and Kavedžija 2015, 17 as cited in Ortner 2016, 59). Bringing the two together, Ortner asks, "How can we be both realistic about the ugly realities of the world today and hopeful about the possibilities of changing them?" (2016, 60). Ortner's response, which I saw reflected in the work of the actors I follow in *Tirana Modern*, calls for returning to cultural critique, rethinking capitalism, and applying the basic axiom of practice theory. That is, "if we make the world through social practice, we can unmake and remake the world through social practice" (Ortner 2016, 63). Building on the practice-oriented approach Ortner discussed in an earlier essay (1984), the main social practices I trace in this account are those that surrounded the circulation of books within a part-localized, part-dispersed, and part-imagined community based in Tirana.

From a Suitable Place to a Point without Surface

My entry into the field of Albanian literary production reaches back to December 2008, when I spent a memorable afternoon in a Tirana bookstore (fig. 0.1). The store was located on a single-block street in a prestigious area of the city. In the first room as you entered, the walls to the left and right were lined with floor-to-ceiling shelving. There the work of elite Albanian authors sat spine to spine with a good selection of world literature in translation. A few steps farther in was a compact coffee bar decorated in a style that recalled the city's Ottoman past. Here a dozen or so patrons sat working alone or talking together in spirited tones. Between the books and the conversation, the atmosphere in the shop appealed to my research interest in the ethnography of reading.[15] At the time I was just visiting, but I made a mental note of the place for future reference.

That future came in 2015. After securing institutional clearance "to examine Albanian literary culture from an anthropological perspective," I returned to Tirana with an open-ended research question and the idea of a field site where I could go to collect the empirical evidence I would need to answer it. The question was, "What can the ethnography of reading contribute to cultural analysis in contexts of pronounced social change?" And though the site, as might be expected in a context of change, is no longer what it was when the research began, the personal relationships I established there during my first days of fieldwork provided the basis for a project that would continue over six summers (2015–2019 and 2021), resulting in this book.[16]

With its coat of pale green paint on the outside and its Albanian books and Turkish furniture inside, the bookstore in 2015 occupied several rooms

FIGURE 0.1. Exterior of the bookshop E për-7-shme.
All photos by the author except as noted.

FIGURE O.2. Issue of the journal *E për-7-shme.*

of a detached house, or *shtëpi private*, constructed in the Tirana vernacular style of the 1920s. Located on the border between Ish-Blloku (the once-restricted residential quarter of the former Communist Party elite) and Qyteti Studenti (the area adjacent to the campus of the University of Tirana), the building itself dated to the time of Ahmet Zogu, the leader of Albania from 1922 to 1939.[17]

Set in an urban landscape now dominated by socialist-era apartment blocks and postsocialist high-rises, the property has belonged for generations to the family of Ervin Hatibi, a poet of local renown whose first volume of verse was published, when he was just fifteen years old, under the ideological strictures of the Albanian socialist censors. But though his writing career began under communism, Hatibi came of age as an artist in what he later called "the free Albania of the 1990s" (2019, 380). He has since achieved recognition in the annals of Albanian literature as one of a dozen or so "contemporary poets of note" (Elsie 2005, 198).

In 2004, the poet, then thirty years old, converted the inside hall and small backyard of his family's reprivatized home into a bookstore that became a magnet for Tirana intellectuals. In 2008, he moved abroad. Since then, the businesses operating from No. 1 Rruga Jul Variboba have changed ownership several times.[18] Each successive owner made certain changes to the original conception of the place. But they all preserved its unusual name: E për-7-shme.

FIGURE O.3. Ataol Kaso and Arlind Novi in Tirana
around 2012. Photo courtesy of Pika pa sipërfaqe.

The Albanian adjective *e përshtatshme* (or *i përshtatshëm*, depending on the gender of the noun it describes) means suitable or fitting. With the number seven (*shtatë*) representing the base word, an Albanian reader may appreciate the added sense of something that recurs "every seven" (as the word *ditë*, or day, becomes *e përditshme*, daily). For another, perhaps smaller subset of readers, the bookstore's name will recall the title of the avant-garde literary journal that Hatibi and fellow Tirana poets Rudian Zekthi and Agron Tufa cofounded in 1992.

The journal *E për-7-shme* (fig. 0.2) only went to four numbered issues but has enjoyed something of a cult reputation in Tirana literary circles. As Besar Likmeta noted in a 2011 feature for *Balkan Insight*, "the spirit of the journal, a space where ideas out of tune with the times found a temporary home, continues to live on in a book corner named after it" (2011). In a brief account of the relationship between the two E për-7-shmes, Likmeta pointed to a comment, penned by Zekthi and published in the journal's first issue, which still resonated with Tirana's "young literati" twenty years after the journal folded. That prescient motto—*Si të mos mbijetosh*, How not to survive—could well describe the way the two main human actors in the present account, Ataol Kaso and Arlind Novi (fig. 0.3), came to think about their future.[19]

Arlind was originally from Elbasan, a city of approximately 150,000 people located about fifty kilometers from Tirana, due southeast along the road bearing its name (Rruga e Elbasanit, lit. Elbasan's Road). During communism, Arlind's father, a plumber, and his mother, a mechanic, both worked at Kombinati Metalurgjik, a massive (and now mostly abandoned) industrial complex on the outskirts of the old city. After completing secondary school, Arlind moved to the capital to study Albanian language and literature at the University of Tirana. "Living in Tirana was a shock for me," he said. "After one year, I wanted to return home. But my parents said give it more time."[20] Like so many seeking a better life in postsocialist Albania, Arlind knew he had little choice. And though he's told me he never felt completely at ease in Tirana, what's made him stay, he said, was meeting Eli (his wife) and Ataol (his best friend and business partner).

Ataol was born into an artistic family with deep roots in Tirana. His late father, an actor, and his mother, a singer, are both known to the Albanian public. He grew up around Estrada e Tiranës, the "people's theatre" (*teatri popullor*) in the center of Tirana, where his parents met and performed. After a brief experience living abroad (in Switzerland), which he said left him feeling "uprooted," Ataol also went on to attend the University of Tirana, completing a degree in economics. But though he studied subjects such as banking and finance, the passion for reading and books he cultivated since childhood only increased as he entered adult life.

It was on the trail of hard-to-find books that Ataol first went to E për-7-shme, where he met Arlind, who was then working there part-time. Through "endless discussions" about art, politics, religion, and books, the two formed a friendship and later, the publishing company they called Pika pa sipërfaqe (Point without Surface). There is also a good story behind that name, which Arlind and Ataol have been called upon to tell countless times.

"Whenever we encounter a new reader," Arlind said, "they always ask us, 'Why does your publishing house have this name?'"

"Yes," Ataol said. "It's a story we have re-told a thousand times."[21]

In a 2015 interview with Nicola Pedrazzi, a reporter for OBC Transeuropa, for example, Ataol explained (in Italian) that the name could be traced to a conversation "about cosmology."[22] The referenced conversation took place in Elbasan, between Arlind and Rudian Zekthi, the poet and cofounder of the journal *E për-7-shme*, who also happened to be from Elbasan. "I told Rudian we were creating a publishing house," Arlind said, "and that we were having a problem coming up with a name. Rudian said, 'Why don't you call it *pika pa sipërfaqe*?'—which was a euphemism for the Big Bang."[23]

The name Arlind and Ataol chose for their company thus came through Zekthi's translation of the theory Stephen Hawking described in his 1988 book, *A Brief History of Time*, according to which all the matter in the universe was said to have originated from a point so small that it possessed no surface. "We too are small," Ataol said, rounding out Pika pa sipërfaqe's origin story, "and we too would like to be infinitely dense" (Pedrazzi 2015).

A look through Pika pa sipërfaqe's catalogue can give a concrete sense of what Ataol meant.[24] Between the 2009 translation of Kurt Vonnegut's *Slaughterhouse-Five*, which launched their project, and the 2021 publication of *The Complete Fictions* of Jorge Luis Borges (trans. Bashkim Shehu, 2021), some of the other notable authors Pika pa sipërfaqe has published in translation include Hannah Arendt (1906–1975), Zygmunt Bauman (1925–2017), Roberto Bolaño (1953–2003), Italo Calvino (1923–1985), Witold Gombrowicz (1904–1969), Milan Kundera (b. 1929), Simone Weil (1909–1943), James Joyce (1882–1941), Philip K. Dick (1928–1982), and Roberto Arlt (1900–1942). In bringing these and many other literary and intellectual forces into Albanian, Pika pa sipërfaqe has arguably created possibilities "as singular, and as awesome, as great authors themselves" (Borges 1999, 3). Put otherwise, this small press has created new spaces of imagination where "good readers" (in the Borgesian sense of that term) can now go to encounter, transform, and create new ideas, interpretations, memories, dreams, tools, and practices—each the origin points of new translations and social arrangements.

By my last count in 2021, Pika pa sipërfaqe had added 116 titles to the Albanian bookshelf. That number includes twenty-eight original works by Albanian authors and eighty-eight works in translation.[25] To put these numbers in the local context, one of the larger contemporary Albanian publishers, Toena, reported publishing more than 130 books per year since 1993 (Toena 2013). Compared to Toena's staff of around thirty employees, however, Arlind and Ataol have managed the operation of Pika pa sipërfaqe mostly on their own.

"Both of us are doing seven jobs at the same time," Ataol said. "Translator, editor, distributor, salesmen, keeping correspondence with the copyright holders, negotiating with the translators, keeping track of the whole process of printing, pagination, book covers. We're doing all of that. Just two of us. With some very important help from Arlind's brother Orges [Novi] and Eligers [Elezi, a mutual friend]."[26]

The group of translators with whom Ataol referenced negotiating now includes more than fifty individuals with a wide range of secondary linguistic specializations, geographic locations, and areas of expertise. Those who have regularly collaborated with the publishers include both established and up-and-coming writer-translators such as Agron Tufa, Rudi Erebara, Romeo Çollaku, Edlira Lloha, Jonila Godole, Bashkim Shehu, Enis Sulstarova, Primo Shllaku, Balil Gjini, Erion Karabolli, Elvis Hoxha, Blerta Hyska, and Arben Dedja. Working in collaboration with Pika pa sipërfaqe (along with a handful of other Tirana-based publishers), this broad collective has brought into Albanian a range of books corresponding with their interests and expertise, written mostly but not exclusively by American, Latin American, and European (especially Central European) authors who were banned, censored, or otherwise unknown in Albania during communism.

To secure the rights to publish these works and to obtain the funds to pay the translators, Pika pa sipërfaqe's "work-net" has extended to many international institutions and agencies, including the Polish Book Institute in Kraków, the Sur Translation Support Programme in Buenos Aires, and the Wylie Agency in New York. For printing and cover art, Arlind and Ataol have maintained long-term relationships with fellow Tirana residents Edi Vathi of West Print, a local printing company specializing in book production, and Erzen Pashaj, an independent artist who was a friend from the early days at the bookstore.

Pika pa sipërfaqe's main distribution networks start from—and circle back through—the social media accounts Arlind and Ataol have managed on Facebook and Instagram. These accounts are now connected to thousands of readers around the world, hundreds of physical bookstores in the Western Balkans, dozens of online sellers with local and international reach, frequent book fairs organized with community partners in Tirana, and the national book fairs held annually in the capitals of Albania, Kosovo, and North Macedonia.

The book fairs are important not just as opportunities to sell books and make some money (although they are that too) but also to talk with people and to be in touch with readers. The publicity the fairs generate also feeds into each of the preceding circuits—through direct contact with readers and booksellers and through multimedia exposure in newspapers, magazines, television, and various online media.

To provide a concrete illustration of the publishers' "global reach," I recently searched "Pika pa sipërfaqe" on OCLC WorldCat, "the world's largest network of library content and services." The search returned

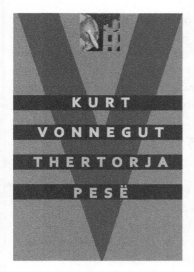

FIGURE 0.4. Book cover for
Thertorja pesë, published in 2009.
Courtesy and © Pika pa sipërfaqe.

a list of twenty-six books, often with multiple copies, belonging to the collections of major research libraries located in the United States, Germany, Poland, Sweden, and the Netherlands. As a biblio-ethnographer, I wanted to follow the trail of those books to see precisely how they made their way around the world.

When I asked Ataol if he knew how their books ended up abroad, he said yes and named two book distributors, Botimpex and Shtëpi e librit. "The former specializes in selling academic texts to university libraries," he said. "The other selling anything to anyone, including libraries."[27] He then showed me a letter of request, which he planned to oblige, from Stefan Kreutzchmar of the German National Library: "We shall be grateful if you will provide free specimen copies of these [works by Sigmund Freud, Niklas Luhmann, and Georg Trakl] and future media works for our collection."

Another example I was able to trace reaches back to 2012, when Timothy Shipe, a bibliographer for the University of Iowa Libraries and an associate of the UI Center for the Book, traveled to the Balkans "to establish mutually beneficial relationships with booksellers, cultural institutions, and individual writers in the region, and to acquire books for the University Libraries through purchase and donation" (Shipe 2012). Of his experience in Albania, Shipe wrote,

> Virtually all of my purchases were from Tirana's only antiquarian bookstore, E për-7-shme, whose owner Arlind Novi is also a publisher, and is extremely knowledgeable about the history of Albanian literature and publishing.[28] Arlind was able to find over fifty volumes by former IWP [International Writing Program] participants, including nearly complete runs of three journals edited by those writers. When he learned that Kurt Vonnegut had lived and taught in Iowa, he donated a copy of one of his own publications, an Albanian translation of *Slaughterhouse-Five*. (fig. 0.4; Shipe 2012)

On the strength of their editorial choices, the high quality of their work, and their active involvement with local writers and cultural institutions, Pika pa sipërfaqe quickly became one of the most respected names in Albanian publishing. This is not just my opinion but something I came across many times during fieldwork in Tirana. Beyond fieldnote evidence, there are plenty of public sources to support this claim. For example, when Albin Kurti (2017), now serving as Prime Minister of Kosovo, visited the annual Prishtina Book Fair in 2017, he posted the following text (in Albanian) on his own social media accounts:

> Today we were visiting the Book Fair in Prishtina. There we visited the publishers' booths and learned about new publications and reprints. Our government will intensively support publishers, for the translation of quality literary and theoretical works, and for the publication of local authors. The book is an irreplaceable foundation of culture. It was by disrespecting books that we ended up with these ignorant and thieving rulers. We visited with great interest the stands of publishing houses from Kosovo and Albania and met authors and translators from the publishers "Koha" [Time], "Buzuku" [the surname of the first attested Albanian author], "Pika pa Sipërfaqe," etc. One of the publications worth mentioning is the second volume of *Publikes Shqiptare* [Albanian Public], from the publishing house "Zenit" [Zenith]. There you can find important texts for the ideal formation of *Vetëvendosje* [Self-Determination]! (Kurti 2017)

Kurti's descriptions of books—as foundations of culture, antidotes to corruption, and mediators of new group formations—anticipate some of the main themes I trace in the chapters that follow. And though the first two publishers he mentioned were based in Kosovo and did not come up in my conversations about publishing in Tirana, the other two seemed to come up whenever it was a question of who was publishing serious authors, ensuring quality translations, respecting copyright, using quality paper, and so on.

The response of Enis Sulstarova, a prolific sociologist and one of Pika pa sipërfaqe's frequent collaborators, was characteristic of the sorts of opinions I heard from many in the field. "They're doing good work," he said, referring to Arlind and Ataol. "Educating the readers here. They know good books, things that are not well known here, and people are reading that now."[29] Ylljet Aliçka, a successful novelist and short story writer had a similar view, though he added a note of concern that was also repeated by many. "I respect Pika pa sipërfaqe," he said. "But I'm concerned. They do excellent work but won't compromise like the big publishers."[30]

This was a legitimate concern, which both Arlind and Ataol shared. Most of the books in their catalogue have been well received. But none have been financially profitable. In Librari Alba, one of several upmarket bookstores in the city center, "where all the new publications of local and foreign authors are found," there was a dedicated shelf for Pika pa sipër-faqe. It was not prime real estate, but it was there, and up to date with the recently published titles. I asked the bookstore attendant if those books were popular. "No, not popular," she said. "But good. Some people find them online or by the title," she continued. "But it's a new publisher and a small publisher."[31]

As I write this in late 2021, the publishers are facing serious difficulties. They have paid a high price for their independence. But contrary to the motto of the journal that brought them together, so far, they have sur-vived. "Now is a difficult time in terms of money," Arlind said. "But we are resisting."[32]

Story and Theory

What can an ethnographer make from this story of two readers turned publishers in a postsocialist city? To find out, I pursued the strategy that Lila Abu-Lughod, in her essay "Writing Against Culture," called, "writing ethnographies of the particular" (Abu-Lughod 1991, 149–57). What first drew me to the approach Abu-Lughod suggested was simply that the heu-ristic of "Albanian culture" seemed inadequate to the task of understand-ing and conveying what life was like for Arlind and Ataol. To begin with, they were living in a world permeated with global flows and an onrush of postsocialist reinvention. Moreover, they were exquisitely aware of the dangers of generalization and the violence of abstraction. As publishers working in a highly politicized field, they cultivated a professional reflex-ivity and were careful in choosing the words they used to describe them-selves. By their own account Arlind and Ataol were two friends who met by chance and went on to cofound a not-for-profit publishing company. They worked together, they said, not for money or prestige but "to keep reading and discussing good books." The solution they devised for this purpose was to establish a small press, which they have described as "an independent, social project dedicated to publishing foundational works of literature, philosophy, and criticism."[33]

But what did being *independent* mean to Arlind and Ataol? In what sense was their project *social*? And what, in their view, made a literary work *foundational*? If I wanted to understand the particular meanings and values Arlind and Ataol attached to their actions, I would need to assimilate—as much and as best as I could—their perspectives of Albanian modernity and everyday life in Tirana. In that regard, Alisse Waterston's (2019) notion of "intimate ethnography" provided a helpful model for how to move outward from immersion in other people's lives to "being broad, comparative, and holistic; moving toward understanding; and attending to the conditions and possibilities of human social life" (2019, 9). The notion of intimate ethnography Waterston first developed with Barbara Rylko-Bauer (2006) was different from the work I did in Tirana insofar as their concept referred to working with source material that was directly connected to an ethnographer's closest family relations, such as one's own mother, father, or grandparent. However, I think the general idea of looking squarely at a particular "lived life" as a way to "grasp history and biography and the relations between the two within society" (Waterston 2019, 8) can work well when applied thoughtfully and rigorously to other kinds of research and writing that demand intimacy between the participants involved in generating the account.[34]

Much as the dialectic thinking that animates intimate ethnography suggests a way to move from biography to history, Robert Darnton's "general model for analyzing the way books come into being and spread through society" (1982, 67) offers a useful framework for understanding how a network of readers, writers, translators, and publishers interacted with and influenced one another through the action of a set of shifting social, economic, political, legal, intellectual, and ethical norms. Darnton's model operated from the premise that "the parts [of a circuit of communication] do not take on their full significance unless they are related to the whole" (67). Taking a holistic view of books as a medium of communication, Darnton showed that it was possible for historians to relate activities accomplished at particular points in a circuit of books to activities accomplished at other points in the same circuit. Once the related agencies of authors, publishers, printers, sellers, and readers were seen also to be related to the broader "elements in society" through which books moved, Darnton argued, "historians can show that books do not merely recount history; they make it" (81).

Together with these perspectives from intimate ethnography and the history of books, the biblio-ethnography I did in Tirana also drew from theories in literary, media, and urban anthropology.[35] Because books are media and cities are centers of attraction for writers and publishers, I was able to combine elements from social studies of writing, analyses of mass media and communication, and the anthropological study of city life into a single analytical frame. In the spirit of Pierre Bourdieu's (1993) analysis of the field of French literature in the Second Empire (based in Paris), and Sherry Ortner's (2013) interpretation of the independent film scenes in neo-liberal America (based in New York and Los Angeles), I brought together (in Tirana) a social analysis of literary production, cultural research on the practices of media makers and users, and direct engagement with city life and urban space.

Returning to the idea of the book as a medium and a technology, one of the special properties of printed books is their *durability*. My choice to italicize the last word of the previous sentence, for example, will stand as an index of the enduring materiality of book design and typography for as long as this book stays in circulation. There is a paradox hidden here, however, which anthropological and literary studies of books as objects can make clear: The meanings and values people ascribe to books are not fixed by the materiality (Miller 2005) or textuality (Warner 1990) of print. On the contrary, what books mean—what they say—can change along with the circumstances in the lives of the people who produce, distribute, consume, discard, salvage, and repurpose them.

To substantiate this claim, I took up Arjun Appadurai's broader sugges-tion to "follow the things" (Appadurai 1986a, 5). Tracing the metaphor-ical life cycle of books through websites, warehouses, coffeeshops, book fairs, street markets, private meetings, public readings, and more, I came to see the publishing house as a kind of knot or network (Latour 1993, 3–5) through which local and global histories, meanings, and imaginaries intersected, acted on one another, and mobilized new and yet to be deter-mined ways of being, thinking, and acting. In Latour's social theory, actors of any scale (from a small press to the world market) are both "*made* to act by many others" (Latour 2005, 46) and *made up* of a series of local "inter-actions," "conversations," "pieces of paper," "exchanges," and "arrange-ments" (Latour 1993, 120–21). In keeping with this perspective, the key actor in the present account is the publishing house itself.

The image of Pika pa sipërfaqe I want to convey—almost literally a point without surface—is thus not a thing but an event, something that happens, that comes into being and is constituted through the fleeting and enduring associations of writers, readers, translators, poets, artists, activists, organizers, and the rest. When I speak of Pika pa sipërfaqe as an actor, therefore, it is not to collapse all distinctions between the existence and agency of humans and nonhumans; it is instead to emphasize how social relations can be sought, created, and transformed through the practices and equipment of literary production.[36] So even as I acknowledge that there could be no books without a long list of mundane things like paper, glue, ink, and words, I want it to be clear that my biblio-ethnographic interest in Pika pa sipërfaqe starts from and returns to the same point: the individual people, living their particular lives, that this small press operating on the margins of Europe has mobilized within and across Albania's national boundaries.

Subject, Informant, Interlocutor, Friend

The present work began from the two generalizable conclusions of my previous project (Rosen 2014, 189–95). These were, first, that there was nowhere an abstract reader, readership, or reading public; and second, that as far as ethnography was concerned, the topic of reading worked better as a point of entry than as an object or unit of analysis. Carrying these ideas with me to Tirana, I used the methods of participant observation and interview to learn from a few people I got to know well how reading created social contexts and relationships that otherwise would not exist.

The method I used—talking with Arlind and Ataol about Cervantes, Dostoyevsky, Proust, Gombrowicz, Kundera, Bolaño, and the rest—produced new contexts and relationships, mediated by literature, that I would have been unlikely to access by other means. Even a few questions about their reading practices opened the way to several hundred hours of participant observation. This yielded many more thousands of words of direct and indirect testimony.

Building the rapport this kind of research required was not effortless or inevitable, but it helped that I could mobilize a side of myself that enjoyed talking about the kinds of books the "subjects" of the ethnography published. That I genuinely respected my "informants" also helped. Subject, informant, interlocutor, friend. Anthropologists use many terms—all of them problematic for different reasons—to refer to the people they depend on to write their ethnographies.

In the following pages, I often call Arlind and Ataol interlocutors. This is because what we did together most was talk. The focus of our conversations was the publishing house. In that regard, my interest was shared by many Tirana observers. But for a long time now, I think the more accurate term for me to use would be "friends." What else do you call someone you have known and liked for many years, who you think of fondly and care about, whose words and actions would seem to reciprocate your expressions of concern and affection? This is the definition of a friend, and though writing ethnography complicates any simple designation, this is how I see Arlind and Ataol. As I wrote in one of my notebooks on June 30, 2017:

> Despite the fieldwork angle, I think genuinely at this point, these are my friends, and I interacted with them as such. We did get to some discussion of their work. And I learned some basic facts. They have been busy. Published twelve books in 2016 and are on pace to publish at least as many in 2017.

The proximity here of the personal (these are my friends) and the professional (they published twelve books) underscores my dual attachments: first, to Arlind and Ataol; and second, to their work. Re-reading my notebooks I can recognize how invested I have been in seeing them succeed. My decision to construct a field around our initial encounter stemmed from the value I immediately and viscerally ascribed to their editorial vision. And though I do not wish to overstate the significance that reading the likes of Borges and Bolaño may have for an abstract Albanian public, I do hope to show that tracing a network through this field of literary translation is worthwhile—not least for what it can make visible about the role of publishing and reading in the major processes of Albanian modernity— including urbanization, modernization, nationalism, capitalism, socialism, and globalization.

But before proceeding with the account, I want to say a few more words about my positionality and access.[37] In her own methodological remarks on (attempting to do) fieldwork in Hollywood, Sherry Ortner wrote, "There are really two distinct issues of access for the anthropologist. One has to do with the possibility of participant-observation; the other with obtaining interviews" (2009, 175). As a contribution to the wider field of media production studies, Ortner introduced the term "interface ethnography" to describe doing participant observation "in the border areas where the closed community or organization or institution interfaces with the public" (176). To characterize what it was like trying to obtain interviews from Hollywood filmmakers—who Ortner saw as being "not that much different from anthropologists and academics"—she used the term "studying sideways" (176).

Like Ortner, I did some productive interface ethnography for this project—for example, at book fairs and book talks. But in contrast to the experience Ortner described, it was not very hard for me to access the inner spaces of book publishing in Tirana. Indeed, the community attached to Pika pa sipërfaqe was remarkably open to the intrusions of my practices of participant observation. As for the question of studying sideways, there was no doubt that the members of the publishing collective and I shared mutual intellectual interests. This was apparent from my discovery—at the book fair where I met Arlind and Ataol for the first time—of Pika pa sipërfaqe's translations of foundational works by Pierre Clastres (*Society against the State*), Hobsbawm and Ranger (*The Invention of Tradition*), and Tzvetan Todorov (*The Conquest of America*). But I'm not sure it would be accurate to say that the members of this community were "very much part of the world that we as academics inhabit" (Ortner 2009, 183). Rather than studying sideways, then, I would characterize my project as studying sideways *with a difference*.

Yes, my interlocutors knew anthropology very well. And yes, they were as interested in my take on Malinowski and Lévi-Strauss as I was in their views of Migjeni and Kadare. All else being equal, I would assume that an assistant professor based at a public university in small-town America who was researching respected book publishers in a European capital was probably studying up. Yet, in Albania, where the average wage in 2019 was less than one hundred dollars a week (Laurenson 2019), that assumption breaks down fairly quickly. So while I was able to secure research funds by convincing grant makers that Pika pa sipërfaqe mattered, the ones who were doing the work I said mattered were facing mounting financial stress and uncertainty. I knew because I had the wherewithal to spend one to two months with them every summer.

But it is possible, I think, for fieldworkers to get away from the whole question of studying up, down, or sideways—with or without a difference. In my own ongoing effort to cultivate an "ordinary ethics" of ethnographic practice, I take my cues from the anthropologist Michael Jackson.[38] In the preamble to his exploration of the life stories of Emmanuel Mulamila, Roberto M. Franco, and Ibrahim Ouédraogo, Jackson explains (2013b, 13):

> Methodologically, then, an anthropology of ethics seeks to locate ethics within the social. . . . This implies a focus on . . . the extraordinary stories of *ordinary* people . . . whose experiences bring into sharp relief the ethical quandaries, qualms, and questions that all human beings encounter in the course of their lives.

As Jackson's work suggests, we *all* would do well to "dissolve our conventional concepts of the social and the cultural into the more immediate and dynamic life of intersubjectivity—that is, the everyday interplay of human subjects, coming together and moving apart, giving and taking, communicating and miscommunicating" (Jackson 2013b, 9). More specifically, as a matter of methodology, these everyday ethics "effectively reinscribe the role of ethnography as a method for exploring a variety of actual social situations before hazarding generalizations" (11).

In this spirit of ordinary ethics, there is one last side of myself I want to disclose. When I first traveled to Albania, in 2006, it was not for research but for love. It was Smoki who brought me to E për-7-shme in 2008, and Smoki again who facilitated my introduction to Arlind and Ataol in 2015. At that first meeting I remember marveling at the way the young publishers seemed to read a whole life history into her family name. And though I later noticed that it was not uncommon for Tirana people to try to place someone based on a few quick questions about their mother's or father's name or where their relatives lived before migrating to the capital, in the case at hand, the story was more legible.

Smoki's paternal grandfather, Shevqet Musaraj (1914–1986), emerged as a writer during Albania's National Liberation Movement (1942–1945). He was probably best known as the author of the satirical poem *Epic of the National Front* (1944), which he wrote when he was the editor of the anti-fascist magazine *Exercising Freedom* (Buda and Lloshi 1985, 729). The layers of meaning behind this association followed me through the project. When Arlind or Ataol introduced me to other members of their community, for example, they would often present me in roughly these terms: Meti, foreign anthropologist, husband of the granddaughter of Shevqet Musaraj. Generally, I thought the connection helped me to establish a little bit of social capital among a network of people who respected writers and books. But given the extreme politicization of the literary field in Albania, there were likely also times when it had the opposite effect.

Organization of the Book

Tracing associations between people, places, objects, ideas, and institutions, each of the following chapters explores a set of related questions about what people do with books and what books do with people.

The first chapter, "One Hundred Years of Transformation," provides a concise overview of Tirana's social and urban development—from a small town with an Ottoman past to a modern capital with a European future. The chapter also provides a basic orientation to the field of contemporary book publishing in Albania and a condensed history of Albanian literature.

Chapter 2, "Miracles of the Street," approaches the observable circuit of books in Tirana as both a literal (semiotic) and figurative (back-of-the-book) index of Albanian modernity. The account starts from a ground-level description of Tirana's layered history as it is made visible in the old books that are sold on the city's streets. Through an analysis of books as commodities, anthropological traces, and technologies of imagination, the chapter establishes the social and material situation in which book publishing in the Albanian capital occurs. Adopting the term *mrekullitë*, or miracles, which one of my interlocutors used to describe the best and rarest treasures to be found in Tirana's outdoor book markets, I look to the movement of books in this chapter as a way to get at theories of action proposed by ordinary actors—that is, what Latour (2005, 50–52) called "practical metaphysis." Following lines of connection from the books on the street to those in Pika pa sipërfaqe's catalogue, the chapter shows the publishing house to be a point of dense intersection, bringing together local and global histories, meanings, and imaginaries.

The third chapter, "In the Public Interest," traces a structure of feeling from the very beginnings of Albanian literary production in the sixteenth century to the twenty-first century formation of the publishing collective Pika pa sipërfaqe. Drawing on a variety of historical and ethnographic sources, the discussion in this chapter considers the publishers' critique of past and present social conditions, their vision of a better future, and their belief in publishing as a means of social transformation, both in the contemporary context and in conversation with other socio-literary projects—especially the Albanian *Rilindja* (lit. rebirth) in the nineteenth century and the twentieth century's Albanian Socialist Realism.

Chapter 4, "Reading Nearby," advances the book's core argument that literary activity is always also social activity. The chapter builds up a theory of reading as a form of collective action that is driven by social relationships and social objectives. To substantiate this perspective, empirical examples drawn from fieldwork in Tirana show how specific acts of co-reading contributed to the emergence of a new literary community. The broader intention of this chapter is to demonstrate the application of the general approach I call reading nearby.

The fifth chapter, "Between Conflicting Systems," shows how a grinding of discordant value systems produced the more general paradox that I describe as *ordinary tragedy*. The analysis in this chapter reaches back to the structure of feeling that runs through the history of Albanian literature to make sense of my interlocutors' decision to hold onto values and social ideals that they understood to be at odds with what people must do to survive in contemporary Albania. Starting from the impulse to learn how two local booksellers made sense of the contradictory systems of meaning operating in their everyday lives, the chapter examines the complexities of social and economic life in Tirana at a time when old and new moral economies routinely clashed with the capitalist principle of profit.

In the outline I included with a proposal for this book, I left room for unexpected outcomes to emerge from the dual trials of writing the ethnography and "registering the effects of the written account on the actors" (Latour 2005, 135). I described my plans to return to Tirana in summer 2020, where I imagined I would have the opportunity, in conditions similar to the ones in which the fieldwork took place, to enroll Arlind and Ataol in some "dialogic editing" (Feld 1987). That was in December 2019, a time that coincided with the outbreak of a new virus that "engulfed an unprepared world" (Yan et al. 2020). The present account was thus mediated by the pandemic that continued into the time of writing. And though this was not part of the original research design, the conversations-at-a-distance (conducted via WhatsApp and Gmail) that I was able to bring into the conclusion, "A Good Time to Read," serve to underscore the situated, empirical, and intersubjective—that is to say, ethnographic—truth and reality of the social situation that this biblio-ethnography made visible.

One Hundred Years of Transformation

The first historical nucleus of the town emerged and grew together with the old Mosque of Sulejman Pasha at the center of the present-day structure of the city, just at the crossroads of the main arteries of the interregional trade transit. Together with the mosque . . . other buildings were erected, including those of feudal lords and their relatives on the right bank of the Lana stream. . . . At a distance of 50–60 meters west of the mosque, they built a bakery, a bath and an inn, three service facilities that influenced the expansion of the bazaar. These buildings, together with the dwelling houses, barns, courtyards, wells, green groves, lanes, squares and graves . . . [formed] an entity of sociological, property, gender and family connections not only at the time of their emergence, but also very long afterwards.

— ALIAJ, Lulo, and Myftiu, *Tirana*, 14

Placing Tirana, Capital of Modern Albania

In the last one hundred years, Tirana has been transformed from a small town with an Ottoman past to a modern city with a projected future in the European Union.[1] In 1920, when the Congress of Lushnjë made it the capital of a newly independent state, the public life of Tirana's roughly 15,000 inhabitants took place within an area of three-square kilometers (Aliaj et al. 2003, 28). Why, then, did the Congress choose this place to be the capital?

Much like the idea of the nation itself, the blueprint for Tirana's future was first drawn in the pages of a political manifesto.[2] In his 1899 book *Albania, What Was It, What Is It, and What Will It Be?*, the author and activist

Sami Frashëri wrote, "The center of Albania, that is, the general capital, should be one of the cities that are located in the middle of the country and where the Albanian language will be spoken" (Frashëri 1899, 69) Such a city, Frashëri continued,

> will be arranged in the most beautiful shape, with wide and straight roads, with nice houses, squares and everything necessary; it will be enlarged and increase in a short time because all the Albanian elite and the intellectuals of the country will get together and build their houses there . . . and since its inhabitants would be from all parts of the country, the language of the city will be a mixed and cultivated one, so that it can be used as a general and literary language throughout all of Albania. (69)

The city Frashëri imagined came remarkably close to the reality of the modern capital. Located in the geographic center of the country, the official population of Tirana in 2020 was 895,160 (INSTAT 2020b). If Tirana in 1920 was a compact "entity of sociological, property, gender, and family connections" (Aliaj 2003, 14), Tirana today—mixed and cultivated—has become the undisputed center of Albanian cultural life. Frashëri's book, I would argue, helped to bring about that change.

According to Besnik Aliaj, Keida Lulo, and Genc Myftiu, the old mosque of Et'hem Bey and the Tirana clock tower symbolize "the historical visual memory" of the old city that did not survive the destructions of war and time (Aliaj, Lulo, and Myftiu 2003, 18). In two photographs I took from a similar vantage point near the historical center of Tirana in 2019 and 2021 (fig. 1.1 and fig. 1.2), you can see how the urban landscape behind the symbolic center of the city is changing. Part of the visible difference in the pictures has to do with the time of day: the photo from 2019 was snapped in the evening, when people were coming out to socialize, whereas the photo from 2021 was taken in the morning, when people were on their way to work. But behind the structure of the summer day, the new construction that is visible in the 2021 photo provides a clear index of my interlocutors' vision (reported in Chapter 3) of how the neoliberal state is colonizing everyday life in the city, replacing the old public spaces with a proliferation of new private projects.

Returning now to the foundation of the modern state, by 1931 Ahmet Zogu (then King Zogu I) had mobilized international aid and a team of architects and engineers from Italy and Austria "to make Tirana a modern

European city" (Aliaj, Lulo, and Myftiu 2003, 40). During the Italian occupation of 1939 to 1943, the Albanian capital for the first time took on the appearance of a "rationally planned" (i.e., Fascist) urban center. According to the plan, Tirana was to be populated by Italian citizens and colonial administrators (Aliaj, Lulo, and Myftiu 2003, 42–46). The possibility of realizing that imagined future ended abruptly, however, in September 1943, when Mussolini surrendered to Allied forces and the Nazis took over Tirana. A little over a year later, on November 17, 1944 (Liberation Day), the Albanian partisan forces regained control of their city. They set up a provisional government with the former schoolteacher Enver Hoxha as head of state.[3]

For forty years, the Albanian communist regime engineered a cult of personality around their leader, who ruled the country until his death in 1985. But back in 1946, when Tirana was first made the capital of a "people's republic," the majority of the city's roughly 75,000 inhabitants could not read or write. Having imbibed the basic tenets of Marxism-Leninism, the Party leaders knew that to build socialism they needed to "remake society and create enlightened workers out of illiterate peasants" (Mëhilli 2017, 6). So, along with other "feats of imagination and engineering," the Communist dictatorship established a book publishing industry that issued by 1960 more than 3,000 titles totaling nearly 30 million copies (Prifti 1978, 133).

Despite its investments in developing institutions of education and culture, the regime's increasingly autarkic policies—splitting first with Yugoslavia in 1948, then cutting ties with the Soviet Union in 1961, and finally breaking relations with China in 1978—strained all sectors of public life to the point of collapse. When the regime ultimately fell, in 1990–1991, the political class responded by establishing a multiparty democracy and reopening the country to the outside world.

In a 1994 report for the *World Policy Journal*, international observer Tina Rosenberg wrote, "Nowhere on earth has life changed more drastically in the last five years than in Albania." Complicating that assertion, she then added, "The old ways of doing business persist: personalist rule, subservience to the big man, political disregard of the law, corruption" (Rosenberg 1994, 85). *Plus ça change, plus c'est la même chose.*

These kinds of generalizations are not uncommon in academic discourse or in everyday talk about Albania's postsocialist transformation. Nor are they without any merit. But to get a clearer idea of what changed and what stayed the same in the field of Albanian book production after the

FIGURE 1.1. View of public life near the historical center of Tirana in summer 2019.

FIGURE 1.2. View of public life near the historical center of Tirana in summer 2021.

1990s, it may be helpful now to pick up and connect four concise accounts of the history and present conditions of Albanian publishing—first, from an excerpt of conversation with Arlind and Ataol in 2019; second through a quick virtual tour of Albania's largest bookseller; third, from a report in the local press from 2013; and finally, from an informant who, being protected by anonymity, was able to put the sharpest point on the matter.

Talking History of Publishing in Albania

In the middle of a long conversation with Arlind and Ataol about the state of literature and publication in contemporary Albania, Ataol offered me the following précis. "Another way to put it," he said, "would be to consider the history. Since the end of World War II, with the formation of the Socialist Republic of Albania, and later on, we never had publishers who established themselves in some sort of intellectual pursuit. We either had state publishers or commercial opportunists. The activity of the state publishers depended on an ideology of the modern state. After that idea collapsed, publishing landed at the feet of the commercial opportunists, who viewed it like a job. They picked it just like they would any other, like if they had dealt in vegetables, they would have become vegetable producers. There were a few exceptions. I don't consider us to be unique. But they are mostly like us, independent, small publishers."[4]

"Before 1945," Arlind said, drawing the perspective farther back, "there were a lot of publishing houses, but the quality and the range of the catalogue was very limited. Publishing in the Albanian language really only started near the end of the nineteenth century. And from that period to 1945, the mainstream publishers only published books to spread Albanian nationalism. There were many translations but few classics. . . . After 1945, the situation was as Ataol said. But after the nineties it was different. Translation flourished."

"So you both agree about the state publishers during communism, but the picture of publishing after the nineties was more complicated?" I said.

"If you want to construct a sort of history or genealogy of book publishing in Albania right after the fall of communism," Ataol said, "you would find that the first major publishers were established by the people who worked in the hierarchy of the old publishing houses [Naim Frashëri and 8 Nëntori] during communism. You either had someone working as an editor there or in the lower part of the hierarchy, like administration, warehouse management, or distribution. These were the main and major publishers that were founded in the first five or ten years after the fall of communism. Along with them there were some very small individual initiatives that you might call what I mean by *botues i pavarur* [lit., independent publisher]."

I will return (in Chapter 3) to Ataol's conception of what it means to be an independent publisher in post-communist Albania. But here, to illustrate what Arlind said about the market for translation, let me refer you to the website of Albania's largest bookseller, Adrion, Ltd. When I first visited the store's home page and clicked where it said "Rreth—About," I read that:

> The establishment of Adrion in 1994 was not a coincidence. It started as a necessity after a period of 50 years, when the foreign press and books were prohibited in Albania. Those that were born and raised in that period were filled with psychological pressure towards foreign literature. . . . Through its various selling points in Tirana and other cities, Adrion fulfills the needs of the Albanian market with books in foreign languages and the major titles of newspapers and magazines from all over the world.

The last time I checked the site, the inventory of books for sale was organized under two broad headings, "Libri i Huaj—Foreign Books" (8,424 titles) and "Libri Shqip—Albanian Books" (11,016 titles). When I clicked to see what was available under the latter heading, I saw on the left-hand side of my screen a dropdown menu for twenty-three separate subject areas, ranging from "*Libra Për Shqipërinë*—Albanian Interest Books" to "*Guida, Harta & Gjeografi*—Travel and Leisure." One of the twenty-three menus was labeled "*Autorë Shqiptarë*—Albanian Authors." There I found 1,104 titles available to purchase online. The remaining 9,912 "Albanian books" were works of translation.

Considering that Adrion is just one of many places where Albanian books in translation can be purchased, I see no reason to doubt Arlind's characterization of publishing in Albania after the nineties. But compared to the exact figures that are available from the time when the state was the exclusive publisher, it is difficult to say with any certainty how many books have actually entered the Albanian market since 1991. Indeed, in a report titled "Chaos in the Book Business," Elona Bedalli, a press officer at the Ministry of Finance and Economy in Tirana, described a market where corruption, informality, and pirating created conditions where even "talking about the book market is not as easy as it seems" (2013). Drawing on the "unscientific" data provided by the Albanian Publishers Association, Bedalli reported the following country totals for 2012: "more than" one hundred publishers, "about" 380 printers, and "approximately" 1,200 to 1,500 titles (Bedalli 2013; SBSH 2012).

Despite my best efforts, I was not able to find any more reliable figures than these.[5] To help me understand why it was so hard to get accurate information about the current book publishing industry in Albania, an informant described a "hypothetical paper importer" who used their family connections to someone in the higher tier of the government to consistently underreport the volume of paper they imported. This meant, for example, that for every million reams of paper counted for tax purposes, two million entered the country. As the beneficiary of this "legitimate crime" the importers could now sell their two million reams to the printers, but to hide the paradox of two million reams sold and only one million imported, the importers would only give the printers a receipt for one million. From here the false accounting gets passed from hand to hand. At the end of the line, even the big booksellers at a place like Adrion cannot publicly declare their numbers. Because the publishers can't. Because the printers can't. Because the importers wanted to cheat, and the top government officials were complicit in this. But despite being complicit in the illegality at one end of the chain, the same government officials have no compunction with prosecuting it at the other end.[6]

The picture of the book business built up by this informant's narration was not flattering. But it was nothing compared to "the asphyxia that afflicted literature and society" under the old regime (Hatibi 2019, 375). To give a better sense of the history of literature that was common knowledge to many of the book readers, writers, translators, and publishers I met in Tirana, I will turn in a moment to the history of literary production in modern Albania, a place where literature has gone in the span of a few generations from being subordinated to achieving national goals, to being made to serve the international ideology of Marxism-Leninism, to being treated like any other commodity.[7] But first, it is worth underscoring here what access to books was like in Albania before the fall of communism.

In terms of sheer numbers, books were available in abundance. But though the number of copies in circulation ran into the millions, the range was very limited. This was due to the extreme centralization of book production and distribution that existed before the nineties. Between 1965 and 1973, for example, the only literary press in the country was Naim Frashëri, named in honor of the Albanian poet and "driving force" behind the Albanian Renaissance at the end of the nineteenth century (Elsie 1995, 226). In 1973, a second press, 8 Nëntori (November 8), split from Naim Frashëri to specialize in nonfiction and political writings.[8]

Until 1991, Naim Frashëri and 8 Nëntori held a complete monopoly over the legal traffic in books in Albania. As Arlind put it (in French) in a 2017 interview with the journalist Louis Seiller:

> Before communism, there were few publishing houses, barely 5,000 [titles] had been published. With the establishment of the state monopoly, censorship hit everything that the regime considered decadent, bourgeois, and contrary to the line of Marxism-Leninism. Foreign works were massively banned. Very few modern classics have been translated. Some had been [translated] but were not published, such as Dostoyevsky or Camus. Despite the censorship, some books circulated secretly thanks to Kosovar editions and people were aware of a few names. After the collapse of the regime and the disappearance of state editions, the number of private publishers exploded. Many wanted to fill this gap. (Seiller 2017)

By the second decade of postsocialism, with the advent of online booksellers, "the world market" of literature finally began to open for readers like Arlind and Ataol. The fall of communism in Albania thus coincided, ironically, with the emergence of a market where, in the words of Marx and Engels, "the intellectual creations of individual nations become common property. National one-sidedness and narrow-mindedness become more and more impossible, and from the numerous national and local literatures there arises a world literature" ([1848] 1998, 39).

Albanian Literature in One Thousand Words

In the preface of his two-volume history of Albanian literature, Robert Elsie depicted his subject as "a tender shrub . . . sprouting in the ruins of its own literary traditions" (1995, ix–x). The first attested Albanian text larger than a single line or short list of words—*The Missal of Gjon*

Buzuku—was written by a Catholic cleric in 1555. What has survived of the book contains sections of the Bible translated into Gheg (the northern Albanian dialect). In the colophon, Buzuku wrote,

> If perchance mistakes have been made in any part, I pray and beg of those who are more learned than I to correct them. For I should not be surprised if I have made mistakes, this being the very first work, great and difficult to render into our language. Those who printed it had great difficulty and thus could not fail to make mistakes, for I was not able to be with them all the time. Running a church, I had to serve in two places. (Elsie 1995, 48)

Thus were the conditions in which Albanian literature first grew. Catholic-inflected, written with a Latin alphabet, and printed in Italy, the earliest forms of Albanian literary production consisted mainly of translations and commentaries on religious texts. Between the collapse of the Counter-Reformation and the rise of Ottoman power in the Western Balkans, these first shoots of Albanian literature withered from general neglect by the close of the seventeenth century.

The eighteenth-century Ottoman-Albanian literature that grew in its place was written in Arabic script, based on Islamic practices, and created a new language that mixed Albanian, Turkish, and Persian idioms. Because the intellectual leaders of the then emergent movement for national awareness associated this second strand of Albanian literature with foreign cultural imperialism, however, the witty and erudite poetry of the *bejtexhinj* (couplet maker) would soon be abandoned in favor of developing a new, Western-facing romantic nationalism.

The nineteenth-century Rilindja literature of the Albanian Renaissance took inspiration—via European mediators such as Johann Georg von Hahn's (1854) *Albanian Studies*—from the ancient oral tradition of Albanian epic verse (Morgan 2016, 102–3). Modern Albanian literature thus turned from themes and styles reflecting its colonial present to ones recalling a mythical past. This turn culminated with the publication of Gjergj Fishta's *The Highland Lute* (1937). Often dubbed "the Albanian *Iliad*," *The Highland Lute* is an epic narration of the Albanian struggle for autonomy. According to Elsie, it constituted "the first Albanian-language contribution to world literature" (1995, 391).

The established precedent of cutting off rather than cultivating the roots of Albanian literature was repeated with force after the communist takeover in 1944. Instead of nurturing the mostly noncommunist writers who emerged during the country's brief periods of independence (1912–1939) and subsequent occupation by Italy and Germany (1939–1944), the new regime led by Enver Hoxha, Koçi Xoxe, and Mehmet Shehu deemed reactionary and anti-patriotic any artist or intellectual—including Gjergj Fishta!—whose work deviated from the doctrine prescribed by Albanian Socialist Realism.

Officially adopted at the Second National Congress of the Writers' Union in 1952, Albanian Socialist Realism adhered to the Soviet model that linked the "truthful, historically concrete representation of reality . . . with the task of ideological transformation and education of workers in the spirit of socialism" (Pipa 1991, 7–8). Noncompliance was subject to sanctions ranging from demotion and relocation to arrest, imprisonment, torture, and execution (Pipa 1991, 18–23). Despite these constraints, a genuine literature again managed to take root, for example, in the best poems and novels of Dritëro Agolli (1931–2017) and Ismail Kadare (b. 1936).[9]

In the calamities that shook the foundations of Albanian culture after the fall of communism, Elsie saw clear indications of the recurring pattern he traced through his 1,000-page history. Writing in the early 1990s, he described the postsocialist literary landscape in the bleakest of terms: "Virtually all Albanian language publishing companies have either gone bankrupt or been shut down. No money, no paper, no ink, no jobs and, worse than anything at present, no hope" (1995, xiii). But true to pattern, it was not long before a new crop of publishers emerged from the ruins of state socialism: Onufri in 1992; Toena in 1993; Çabej in 1994; Aleph in 1996; IDK in 2001; Zenit in 2004; and Pika pa sipërfaqe in 2009, among many others.

While the companies just named also published original works by Albanian authors, more than 75 percent of their collective output consisted of translations. This is another strong indication of how important translation has been for the book publishing industry in Albania. But the link between literary translation and transnational circuits of knowledge and imagination is not something that applies only to small nations. No literature can develop in isolation. And just as the authorized version of the Bible (King James Version) was both a work of literary translation and a "treasure house of English prose" (Lewis 1950, 23), so too was Buzuku's *Missal* not only a work of translation, but also the first Albanian book.

The lines of connection between Albanian readers and the universe of world literature that extended outward from the sixteenth century would be put under severe strain, however, by the ideology of "self-reliance" that developed in the last third of the former Communist dictatorship (Mëhilli 2017, 228). What began after World War II with the persecution of intellectuals seen as representatives of the old regime (Elsie 2005, 162) extended by the 1970s to the condemnation of any "alien ideological manifestations" (Pipa 1991, 33; Prifti 1978, 167). Responding to a 1973 report that young people "wanted to read other kinds of books than those offered to them," the Party boss, Enver Hoxha, for instance, said, "No, comrades . . . We have nothing to learn from this [European, imperialist, revisionist] culture . . . but should discard it contemptuously and fight it with determination" (Pipa 1991, 74).

To the main subjects of the account that follows, the residual effect of that contempt was one of the great tragedies of modern Albanian history. Indeed, of all the statements about the past I recorded as fieldnotes, the ones that spoke of the damage done by "celebratory histories" of the state and "narrow views" of the outside world were among the most frequent and, it seemed, most deeply felt. The essential idea about the future I drew from these notes had two parts: first, that changing the conditions of social life in Albania for the better would require new ways of thinking; and second, that a new kind of literature could help bring about that change. But before returning to Arlind and Ataol and their views of publishing, I want to establish a clearer picture of the actual social and material conditions in which their publishing work took place. To that end, I turn now to the description of an ordinary day in Tirana as I experienced it in summer 2018.

Miracles of the Street

A commodity appears at first sight an extremely obvious, trivial thing. But its analysis brings out that it is a very strange thing, abounding in metaphysical subtleties and theological niceties.

— MARX, *Capital*, Volume 1: Critique of Political Economy

It was late afternoon when I walked through Fan Noli Square, past the Albanian Parliament, to the shaded entrance of the two-story building that has housed the Albanian Academy of Sciences since 1972.[1] Constructed in the second half of the nineteenth century, the building was originally used for family and official receptions hosted by the feudal Toptani family, who "dominated the Albanian capital for 150 years" (Pettifer 2013). The historic structure served as the Royal Palace during the reign of King Zogu I (1928–1939) and as the Presidium of the People's Assembly during the formative years of Albanian communism (1946–1962). Deemed a cultural monument of the highest category in 2016, the building currently holds the distinction of being the last standing structure to have housed an institution of the Albanian state in 1920, when Tirana was proclaimed the capital (Murati 2016).

I had gone there that afternoon to attend a public lecture organized by the recently formed Urban Anthropology Laboratory of Tirana's Institute of Cultural Anthropology and Art Studies (IAKSA).[2] Arriving just ahead of the scheduled start time, I took a seat near the front, on the right side of the central lecture hall. I noted the date, 12 June 2018, in one of the small notebooks I kept in my shirt pocket all that summer. Glancing over my left shoulder, I counted about two dozen others who had come out to hear anthropologist Ger Duijzings discuss his 2016 book, *Engaged Urbanism: Cities Methodologies*, which he coedited with Ben Campkin.[3]

Duijzings opened with some biographical information. He turned to urban studies in 2009, he said, as "a break from the grim focus" of his earlier work on genocide and war crimes during the Bosnian War. But though his vision of urban anthropology was optimistic, that was not to say he took it lightly. On the contrary, the goal of urban anthropology in his opinion was to contribute to creating "better and fairer cities for people to live in." The question of just how to do this—with an emphasis on developing different methods for different cities—provided the main topic of his hour-long presentation.

I filled ten pages of my little notebook with verbatim snippets of the speech. "Embracing the city as a whole." "Diverse, specific, unique, changeable." "Abundant presence of particular phenomena that ask for special explanation." "Getting at change." "Memories, erasures, evictions." "The street as a place of encounter." "Overwriting hegemonic knowledge."

I circled that last phrase, which I thought summarized the main point of the talk: If anthropology, already a marginal discipline, was to contribute to urban studies—a field dominated by architects, geographers, sociologists, and urban planners who only recently began to encourage "thinking through elsewhere" (Robinson 2016)—it would not be by importing grand theories of urbanization, but by developing what Duijzings called "site-specific methods of observation and intervention." Responding directly to the local codes and vernacular realities encountered in the street, such methods allowed each city—Bucharest no less than London, Tirana as much as New York—to become a laboratory for creating and exchanging its own forms of urban knowledge.

I stepped out of the Academy of Sciences as if into a city transformed. Joining in the *xhiro*, or evening walk, along the now considerably cooler pedestrian street that ran from the new Toptani Shopping Center to the (since demolished) National Theatre, the abstractions of the lecture hall became tangible everywhere I looked.[4] I saw old men walking in shirtsleeves, their hands clasped behind their backs; young women in bright summer clothes pushing children in strollers; thin uniformed waiters moving chairs and arranging tables for the coming café crowd; groups of students with their backpacks, looking heavy on their shoulders; couples walking together, laughing, smart phones at the ready.

Looking ahead I saw the endless traffic rumbling along Martyrs of the Nation Boulevard, where the yellow cabbies parked, doors open, chatting and smoking. Through the lens of engaged urbanism these unremarkable kinds of human activity now seemed to be imbued with some deeper significance. But what was I to make of such fleeting perceptions? How was I to connect these quotidian scenes to the questions I had come to explore? What, in short, did any of this have to do with the ethnography of reading in contexts of pronounced social change?

An answer hit me while I was waiting for the traffic light to turn green. Looking across a street built by the Italians in the 1930s, whose present name recalled Tirana's not-so-distant occupation and liberation—a Bakhtinian point "in the geography of a community where time and space intersect and fuse" (Bakhtin 1981, 7)—I saw Mihal, one of the sidewalk booksellers Arlind had introduced me to the previous summer.[5]

Along with dozens of others throughout the city, Mihal's makeshift stand was a fixture in Tirana. As specific and salient as the stray dogs of Bucharest that Duijzings traced in "Dictators, Dogs, and Survival in a Post-Totalitarian City" (2011), the abundant presence of books for sale on Tirana's streets cried out for explanation. That their arrival coincided with the fall of the old regime is apparent from the Prologue of a finely observed book on post-communist Albania:

It was July 1993 . . . Tirana was chaotic and hot. A single traffic light hung in the center of the city, and it did not work. Private cars, illegal three years earlier, raced through the streets, dodging horse carts and blasting kitschy musical horns. Most were third-hand clunkers from Germany; they say Albania is where a Mercedes goes to die. Books by Stalin, Lenin, Marx, and the Albanian dictator Enver Hoxha littered the streets. (Abrahams 2015, 2)

Twenty-five years later, Tirana in summer was still hot and chaotic. But much else had changed. There were working traffic lights on every corner. The proliferation of cars—not to mention trucks, busses, and heavy construction equipment—prevented anyone from driving very fast in most parts of the city. And while the horse carts and musical horns were no longer conspicuous parts of the cityscape, the cars, including but not limited to Mercedes, were mostly up to date. But the books—maybe even some of the same ones, judging by their sun-faded covers!—were still circulating.

Amid the diverse, specific, and unique change that had taken place in

Tirana, books were still abundantly present on the streets. But why? And what did their presence say about everyday life in this former socialist city? What kinds of memories, erasures, and evictions might be revealed by "reading around" these old books?

With these questions still forming in my head, I crossed with the light to say hello to Mihal. Wanting to preserve a visual fieldnote of the still inarticulate idea that occurred to me moments earlier, I snapped a few photos of the books displayed face up on the low wall running along the western edge of Tirana's Parku Rinia, or Youth Park (fig. 2.1). Among the old books, scattered with pine needles, were Enver Hoxha's *Eurocommunism Is Anti-Communism*, Ismail Kadare's *Theft of Royal Sleep*, volumes II and III of a French edition of Marx's *Capital*, Musa Kraja's *The Teacher in the Party Era*, Diana Çuli's *The Circle of Memory*, Flaubert's *Madame Bovary*, Thomas Mann's *Tonio Kröger*, Thor Heyerdahl's *Aku-Aku*, Salverio Strati's *We, Lazzaroni*, Robert Escarpit's *Literatron*, and Friedrich Schiller's *On Naïve and Sentimental Poetry*. These works of fiction and nonfiction by Albanian, French, German, Italian, and Norwegian authors are indicative of the range of books available at Mihal's stall. Except for the French edition of

FIGURE 2.1. A visual fieldnote—Mihal's bookstall.

Marx, the books I just listed were all printed in the original Albanian or in Albanian translation. All but two were originally published or circulated freely in Albania during the communist era. The two exceptions were *Theft of Royal Sleep*, a collection of Kadare's post-communist stories published by Onufri in 1999, and Schiller's foundational essay on poetic theory, which I recognized by the cover, with its yellow letters on a green background, from the catalogue of Pika pa sipërfaqe (trans. Armand Dedej, 2015).

Although one needs to be careful citing Marx in a post-communist context, I used that memorable first line from "The Fetishism of the Commodity and Its Secret" ([1867]1976, 163–77) as an epigraph to this chapter because it also describes the books on Tirana's streets—apparently trivial things, which upon closer examination reveal condensed histories, for example, of a harsh dictatorship, a subsequent mass migration, and the everyday social relations of those who have managed to secure a precarious living from the re-circulation of the moveable possessions that those who have departed (the country or this world altogether) have left behind.

Books as Commodities

Going by the standard definition of a commodity—any item with a use value that also has an exchange value—books present a case that is especially "good to think."[6] Yet, as Trish Travis pointed out in 1999, "thinking about the book as a commodity, as a good that is good for thinking, does not come naturally" (Travis 1999). This is due, she said, not only to the book's deep cultural associations with sacred and literary texts but also to dominant ideas of reading, which "figure the book as an object . . . with meaning that inheres in its contents, rather than in its points of intersection with the culture around it" (Travis 1999).

But for us, now, to see books as commodities, it should be enough to recall that Amazon, the most valuable brand in the world as I write, started life, also about twenty-five years ago, as an online bookseller. And despite all the considerable differences between Amazon and the book trade in Tirana, the initial success of Jeff Bezos's business venture depended on some of the same factors that brought the books to the streets of the Albanian capital in the 1990s. Namely, "the low price that could be offered for books, and the tremendous selection of titles that were available in print" (Grant 2004, 12).

FIGURE 2.2. Abundant, visible, and asking for explanation.

For an analysis of books as commodities, I found it helpful to reach back to Igor Kopytoff's 1986 essay "The Cultural Biography of Things." There Kopytoff established that commodities are produced through cultural processes by noting that

> the same thing may be treated as a commodity at one time and not at another, and the same thing may, at the same time, be seen as a commodity by one person and as something else by another. Such shifts and differences reveal a moral economy that stands behind the objective economy of visible transactions. (Kopytoff 1986, 64)

Each of these statements also applies to second-hand books in Tirana. But before getting into what stands behind their visible appearance, I need to underline the original point I wanted to make—how I came to the topic in the first place. I began with the question of how to do ethnographic fieldwork in the context of a large city. Starting from the recognition that urban sites are "diverse, specific, unique, and changeable" (Campkin and Duijzings 2016, 2), I used urban wandering (Benjamin 1979) as a device to generate a mental list of phenomena that (a) could be found in abundant presence, (b) were visible from the street, and (c) seemed to ask for special explanation.

The list of images that streamed through my thoughts as I walked along the pedestrian street toward Mihal included memories of seeing coffeeshops named for other European capitals—London, Paris, Oslo, Vienna; construction equipment rumbling down neighborhood lanes; electric box street art; "censored" graffiti—for example, at a perpetual construction site on Joan of Arc Boulevard, where someone crossed out the first two-thirds of an imperative that once said, *"Rebelim, Reflektim, Rikri-jim*—Rebel, Reflect, Re-create" (fig. 2.2); missing or severely damaged storm drain and utility hole covers; whimsically decorated "accordion" busses that were made to look like giant versions of the musical instrument that inspired their name; and many different kinds of unexpected conjunctions—for example, a petrol station next to a bookstore, or an optometrist that is also a physical therapist.

It was after running through this mental catalogue of my experience in Tirana that I arrived at Mihal's display of sun-faded books. Looking at the city from an anthropological perspective, all these features of Tirana's urban fabric can be seen to be related in meaningful ways. But given my specific interest in biblio-ethnography, I decided to turn my focus to the circuit of books, and to ask: What needs do the book markets meet? And what do they reveal about the structures of power that organize everyday life in Tirana?

Indexical Values: Markets, Migrations, Miracles

Just as one can locate topics in a book by checking the alphabetical list of subjects printed on its back pages, the books on Tirana's streets point to key events in Albanian social history. In 1992, for instance, when the country first emerged from half a century of harsh dictatorship, it faced an acute paper and book crisis that made it difficult for schools to function. Writing about Tirana at that time, the anthropologist Clarissa de Waal noted that international aid organizations sent large shipments of schoolbooks that were not much use for practical purposes. "These books," she observed, "like many charitable donations, generally ended up for sale on the streets" (De Waal 2014, 54).

During the period of my own fieldwork, I noted plenty of books that came to the street through channels of international development (e.g., *Adventures in English*, the *VOA Special English Word Book*, and multiple volumes of *Essential English for Foreign Students*). What I saw most, however,

FIGURE 2.3. Indicators—international aid and the domestic product.

were books printed domestically (fig. 2.3). Of these, there remained many titles penned by Enver Hoxha, who died in 1985, leaving behind what the writer and translator Bashkim Shehu has called "incursions into every field of knowledge" (Shehu 2001, 185). Hoxha's memoirs and polemics such as *Years of Childhood*, *When the Party Was Born*, *Eurocommunism Is Anti-Communism*, and *The Khrushchevites* exist today—along with the works of Marx, Engels, Lenin, Stalin, Kadare, Agolli, and other mediators of Albanian Socialist Realism—as durable traces that, in Valentina Napolitano's words, "give force to and are animated by . . . lingering histories. They have a life course, they may haunt but also empower, they may be receding or emerging. Certainly, they refer beyond themselves" (Napolitano 2015, 48).

But how do so many books actually "end up" on the street? The sellers I asked said they regularly bought books from the relatives of the deceased and from those about to go abroad. This was a kind of common knowledge among locals. If you knew where to find a used bookseller (a good possibility since the sellers claimed prominent spaces in the city) you could easily arrange to sell whatever books you didn't want or couldn't keep.

It was in this way that the old books on Tirana's streets pointed to the contemporary phase of Albanian migration (King, Mai, and Schwand-ner-Sievers 2005). During the first major wave, in the fifteenth century, Albanians fled in large numbers to the nearby coasts of Italy and Greece. By the early twentieth century, Albanians had established permanent diaspora communities in large cities in Greece, Romania, Egypt, Turkey, Bulgaria, the United States, Argentina, Canada, and Australia. These patterns of migration came to an abrupt halt during the communist regime, when moving abroad was outlawed. Due in part to an accumulation of "migration potential" during the communist era, rates of Albanian migration have increased dramatically since 1990. According to a 2015 report published by the Migration Policy Institute, "the collapse of the socialist system, the immediate opening of the country, and the radical and chaotic transformation of the economy produced massive migration flows as people sought a better future, either abroad or elsewhere in Albania" (Kosta and Kosta 2015). An estimated one-third of the resident population in 1990 left the country in the first wave of post-communist migration. More recently, according to the 2020 report "Albanian Diaspora in Figures," the total number of individuals who left Albania in 2019 was "360,699 inhabitants, or about 12.4 percent of the total population of 2011" (INSTAT 2020a, 26). Where some local people sold their relatives' old books for a small sum, others simply disposed of them in the trash. In either case, the books wound up in the same place—for sale on the street.

If the movement from the bookshelf to the street is a sign of out-migration, the trip from the dumpster to the bookstall is diagnostic of a different kind of structural inequality. To salvage the books that were thrown out, collectors and sellers depended on—and exploited—an informal network of the country's poorest and most marginalized communities: men, women, and children, mostly but not exclusively members of the local Roma and Egyptian communities, who survived by sorting through the city's garbage, looking not just for books but also for bottles and cans, shoes and clothes, bags and electronics, tools, utensils, and much more. Anything at all with re-sale value could be sold at the "market of old things," which despite recurring evictions since 2015, has continued to materialize on Saturday mornings in Tirana's periphery, albeit increasingly farther out and subject to arbitrary police harassment (fig. 2.4).

FIGURE 2.4. Index of things—Saturday morning market.

The next stop for the better-quality books—bought in bulk and sifted; or spotted by discerning eyes and claimed individually—would be at a stand like the one Mihal operated on the border of the park. Once you started to look for these bookstalls, they were everywhere: along the curved balustrade of a bridge over the Lana stream (fig. 2.5), in the shadow of the dilapidated Pyramid of Tirana (once Enver Hoxha Museum, now slated for demolition), in front of the House of Leaves (once a site of secret surveillance, now a tourist-attracting museum), against the construction hoardings that border Skanderbeg Square (Tirana's first historical nucleus, now a site of perpetual reinvention), and on countless narrow lanes and other dusty tributaries feeding into streets with names like Qemal Stafa, Don Bosko, and Siri Kodra.

The books on the street also raised questions about the sellers. Where had they come from? How did they choose this work? And how did they manage to make a living from it? I still don't have the answers to all these questions. Compared to the relatively easy access I had been granted to the inner spaces of book publishing, the sidewalk booksellers were more reticent to let me in. There were at least two reasons for this. The differences in positionality I discussed in the methodological remarks included in the introduction played an important part. But the greater part, I think, had to

FIGURE 2.5. Index of places—biblio-urban landscape.

do with a habitus shaped by the arbitrary threat of harassment, fines, and eviction that the booksellers had to contend with daily.

Considering the justified fear and suspicion that permeated their lives, I could understand why a bookseller like Mihal would be cautious about telling too much to a note-taking foreigner. Being perhaps oversensitive to the feeling that my presence or my questions might create discomfort, I backed off. So while I was able to learn that Mihal had been persecuted during communism, I can't say—because I don't know—the details of his persecution or what that experience was like for him. From where I sit now, at my desk, I see this as a missed opportunity. There was much I might have learned had I been less timid.

Indeed, of all the book-related indices of Albania's transition to capitalism, the life stories of contemporary booksellers were surely among the most poignant. This was true not just of the booksellers whose persecution during communism brought them into the postsocialist era with a structural disadvantage. It was also true for others, such as Hektor Metani, pictured below in 2017 (fig. 2.6), who were respected during communism, with good jobs that they lost in the transformation.

The first time I asked Hektor if I could take his photograph, he said no. That was in 2015. When I saw him again two years later, instead of asking for a photo, I bought an old Albanian-English dictionary with a dark green cover. I paid 500 Lekë (less than five USD). Edited by Ilo Stefanllari and Frida Idirizi, the dictionary was published in 1988 by 8 Nëntori, one of the two state-controlled publishers supervised by the Party and its related Institute of Studies on Marxism-Leninism. Other than a small tear on the spine (which Hektor repaired with a strip of brown electrical tape) the book was in good condition when I bought it and has held up well to frequent consultation.

The next time I passed by Hektor's bookstall, I bought a copy of the late professor Alfred Uçi's 2010 book, *The Philosophy of Don Quixotism*, for 600 Lekë. It's a beautiful book, published by the Albanian Academy of Sciences, manufactured in the printing house Gurten. The graphic design by Enkelejda Misha repurposed Picasso's iconic 1955 sketch of the literary hero and his sidekick, Sancho Panza, for the cover and frontispiece.[7] At 622 pages, it's a heavy book. I paid up front, but since I had a long walk ahead of me and no bag to carry it in, I asked Hektor if I could come back later to collect it.

"Sure," he said, "no problem."

When I came back the next morning, Hektor invited me for a coffee. We went to the Eurolive betting shop that had taken over the old café next to Hektor's spot on the sidewalk. Although the betting places were then as ubiquitous as Tirana's outdoor bookstalls, this was the first (and last) time I entered one.[8]

It was still early in the morning, but the sun was already hot in the sky.

"Raki? Beer? Whiskey? Cigarette?" Hektor was very generous with me.

"No, thank you," I said. "Just the coffee, please."

We sat together for about thirty minutes. I found out he was from Ksamil, in the south. "Before," he said, "I was a member of the Communist Party."[9] He was a teacher of language and literature. "Not just a teacher," he said, "but also a poet." Some of his poetry was published in the newspaper *Drita*, in 1988. When he lost his job in the country's restructuring, he first tried his luck finding work in Greece. When that didn't work out, he migrated to Tirana, where he'd been ever since.

As he told me his story, a friend of his at the next table was drinking *raki* (a grape liquor) and teasing him, calling out "*Komunist.*" Hektor didn't respond to the interpellation of the old Party ideology that followed him into the postsocialist space of the betting shop, outside of which he spent his days sitting on a square of cardboard in the sun, drinking bottled water to stay hydrated and selling old books for a few hundred Lekë apiece.

Our conversation had run its course. But we stayed to watch the end of a football match. It wasn't close. 4–0. I was leaving the country the next day. I still wanted to get his photograph. It was now or never, I thought (mistakenly). So I asked again. This time he agreed.

I say "mistakenly" because I saw Hektor again the following summer. I was cutting through the small lane around the corner from his old stand, running late for a 9:30 appointment at Friends Book House. Hektor recognized me. "*Amerikan!*" he called to me. We greeted warmly. He invited me to drink coffee. But I had to postpone. From then on, Hektor and I would meet often, and he always insisted on buying me a coffee. After several failed attempts to return the gesture, I thought I might be able to even things out by buying a nice book, so I picked one I thought would go for a relatively high price. It was a compact hardcover edition of Engels's (1884) *The Origin of the Family, Private Property and the State*, published by 8 Nëntori in 1970.[10] It was one of 10,000 copies printed that year in the printing house

FIGURE 2.6. Index of persons—Hektor Metani, bookseller.

Mihal Duri.[11] My plan backfired. Hektor refused my money but insisted I keep the book. It's weird, but of all the difficulties I've encountered in the field, trying to figure out how to meet my obligation to reciprocate the gifts Hektor gave me was one of the most vexing. I tried everything, even being assertive, which doesn't come naturally for me, but I never managed to pay him back.

In an earlier draft of this chapter, I wrote, "Maybe next time." But when I returned to Tirana in summer 2021, Hektor was gone. I stepped into the corner pharmacy (which housed a barbershop when I photographed him in 2017) to see if I could get any information on his whereabouts. "Bukanist, Hektor Metani?" I said with a rising intonation. The pharmacist's face dropped. "*Ka vdekur,*" she said. He has died. Three-four months back. "COVID?" I said. No, cancer. I stood a while in the place his books used to be. Tears formed in my eyes but didn't flow. I walked a little way down Rr. Qemal Stafa. Bought a 2018 edition of Sami Frashëri's (1899) manifesto, paying 400 lekë from another veteran of the street.

In place of the debts I was unable to repay, I include here in my English translation a few lines from Metani's poem "Part of the Whole, Named Livadhja."[12]

> The road, ah the road, you can break your neck on it walking, entering Livadhja. The smell of oregano, the song of the bird community, the melody of the waves, which only rivers know how to make, with a musical instrument still unnamed. The sound of footsteps, yesterday's wind and thunder, with pleasure, with relaxation, with emotion. From this point of view, they took revenge for the fatigue of the road, the heat, the empty space.

The range of possible responses this fragment might elicit—about the mountainous landscape of the Ionian coast near the Greek-Albanian border, for example, or about the stylistic conventions of Albanian Socialist Realism, or indeed about the memories and experiences Hektor Metani brought with him to Tirana—these all point to the inexhaustible indexicality of written communication. Here I am reminded of José Ortega y Gasset, who noted in "The Difficulty of Reading" that "Every utterance is exuberant—it conveys more than it plans. . . . The result of this [unpremeditated gift the exuberance of speech provides us] is that *every* text appears to us a mere fragment of a whole X which it is necessary to reconstruct" (1959, 2). Thus in addition to questions about the lives of booksellers, about Albanian migration since the 1990s, and about other aspects of inequality and the informal economy in Tirana, the books I have been talking about in this chapter also of course raise questions for the ethnography of reading.

And though I wouldn't go so far as Ortega, who said reading itself was a utopian task, I can't say I learned very much about the reading experience of the anonymous, transitory people who stopped one day and not another to browse and occasionally to buy a book on the street. What I did learn—from regular reader-collectors like Arlind, Eligers, Orges, and Shpëtim—was that here, in Tirana, the street was a place to go in search of *mrekullitë*, or miracles, as Arlind called the old and rare books that were hard to find, out of print, and certainly not carried by any of the stores. These readers taught me what they learned from their own experience— that it was possible, after all, to find miracles on the street.

From Salvage Operations to Savage Detectives

Lifting the seat of the electric scooter he shared with his brother Orges, Arlind showed me one of the treasures he thought—correctly—would be of special interest to me: Robert Elsie's *Songs of the Frontier Warriors: Albanian Epic Verse* in a bilingual English-Albanian edition. I asked if this book was something he bought for its re-sale value.

"No," he said. "This is for my library of Albanian interest." When I asked Arlind to tell me about the library and how it was organized, he characterized it as stemming from obsession and fear. Obsession for collecting books that could be useful for the future. Fear that the last traces of the old public spaces and institutions—now to be found only in books—were in danger of disappearing forever.

"In America," he said, "if you want to find something, you can go to the library. But here, in Albania, it's not the same. Our public institutions are disappearing. This is why I want to create a rich library, an archive, for the publishing house, for us, for others, for example Smoki, who want to write something. And for personal use, for Ataol. If I had the possibility, I would build a public library."[13]

What Arlind said about his library of Albanian interest—that he wanted to create an archive for the good of the broader community—could also describe what he and Ataol have been doing with their publishing company, Pika pa sipërfaqe. This suggested to me something I had not considered before; it helped me to see the area of overlap between the operations of salvage and translation. In each case, the action involves searching for something (knowledge or practices, meaning or stuff) that needs to be rescued and carried back, recorded, and preserved. Whether that something was in danger of being lost through the violence of modernization at any cost or because it remained inaccessible, in another mode of human communication, the work of salvage and translation have much in common.

Through interactions with Tirana's antiquarian book traders, for instance, Arlind traced associations back through circuits of communication that came to Albania by many routes and through many languages, scripts, and orthographies. In his work with Ataol and the transnational network of agents and institutions they depended on, the trail of associations extended outward in space and time to include the whole world, from antiquity to the present. But though there were clear areas of overlap between the operations of book collecting and literary translation, there were also important distinctions between them. If the criteria for bringing a book into the library of Albanian interest was already implied in its name, the question of how Arlind and Ataol decided which books to publish in translation was not so clear cut.

Given the eclectic nature of their editorial choices, it is probably not possible to answer definitively the question of how Arlind and Ataol decided which books to translate. But at least one of their primary considerations was clear: They sought first to read, then to translate, and finally to publish books that had not yet appeared in Albanian. They were looking to expand, not to duplicate. There was no need, for example, to pursue *Prometheus Bound*, *Don Quixote*, *Gulliver's Travels*, *Madame Bovary*, or *Anna Karenina*. Thanks to dozens of prolific twentieth-century translators such as Fan Noli (1882–1965), Skënder Lurasi (1900–1982), Mitrush Kuteli (1907–1967), Petro Zheji (1929–2015), and Robert Shvarc (1932–2003), these and many more classics of world literature had been established as popular staples among Albanian readers. They can all be found on the bookshelves of Tirana apartments and, as we have seen, for sale on the city's streets.

In addition to not wanting to duplicate works that already existed in translation, there was also the issue of competition with other contemporary publishers. So while I know they would have liked very much to collaborate with someone like Bashkim Shehu or Erion Karabolli on a translation of Roberto Bolaño's 1998 novel, *The Savage Detectives*, Toena beat them to it. This was a pity. At least if I can judge the book by its cover. That the cover art for the Toena edition features an illustration that looks like it came from the result of a Google image search of the term "private detective" suggests to me that not everyone working for the big publisher followed the narrative very closely. For whatever its title might imply, *The Savage Detectives* is not a hardboiled detective story. Benjamin Kunkel, writing for the *London Review of Books*, came nearer to the truth when he said, first, "this book isn't *about* anything," and second, "it's something close to a miracle" (Kunkel 2007).

In a short text titled "On *The Savage Detectives*," Bolaño offered his own précis:

On the one hand I think I see it as a response, one of many, to *Huckleberry Finn*; the Mississippi of *The Savage Detectives* is the flow of voices in the second part of the novel. It's also the more or less faithful transcription of a segment of the life of the Mexican poet, Mario Santiago, whose friend I was lucky enough to be. In this sense the novel tries to reflect a kind of generational defeat, and also the happiness of a generation, a happiness that at times delineated courage and the limits of courage. To say that I'm permanently indebted to the work of Borges and Cortázar is obvious. I believe there are as many ways to read my novel as there are voices in it" (Bolaño 2011a, 353).

Tracing Connections Through a Field of Literary Translation

The titles in Pika pa sipërfaqe's catalog cover a range a styles, genres, locations, and times. The lines of connection between the works are not always obvious to see, but the closer you look, the more interesting the associations there seem to be. To begin with a fairly clear set of connections, a sure line can be traced forward, for example, from Ataol's translation of *Slaughterhouse-Five* in 2009 to his *Breakfast of Champions* in 2015 and Philip K. Dick's generically similar *Valis* in 2017. Tracing a route backward through the catalogue, Arlind suggested another example. He told me that their decision to translate *Etchings of Buenos Aires*—a collection of stories and sketches written by Roberto Arlt and first published between 1928 and 1933 in the Argentine daily *El Mundo*—was inspired by their earlier obsession with Roberto Bolaño.[14] "Let's say, modestly," Bolaño said, confidently, "that Arlt is Jesus Christ" (Bolaño 2011c, 97).[15]

A denser but somewhat more submerged lineage connects Arlt to another one of Pika pa sipërfaqe's favorite authors, the Polish émigré Witold Gombrowicz. This is not just because Arlt's father, like Gombrowicz, migrated to Argentina from present-day Poland. Nor is it only that both Gombrowicz's "Diary" and Arlt's "Engravings" were written while the authors were living in Buenos Aires, nor that their writing first appeared in the periodical press.[16] No. What joined the two authors at a deeper level, along with many others brought to Albania by Pika pa sipërfaqe, was something essential to the quality of their writing: a deeply felt and intensely perceptive critique, often conveyed with recourse to irony and the absurd, of the social realities that structured their lives.

If Arlt came on a recommendation from Bolaño, the route to Gombrowicz came through a book of essays by the exiled Czech writer Milan Kundera. Arlind first read an excerpt of Kundera's 1993 book *Testaments Betrayed* in unauthorized Albanian translation that appeared in *Aleph*, a now defunct literary journal founded by Gentian Çoçoli and published in Tirana. The *Aleph* translation was done by Balil Gjini, an Albanian poet, prose writer, and translator. When Arlind contacted Gjini to express interest in publishing the entire book, Gjini explained that he had already attempted to publish his translation with another publisher, but that publisher failed to get the copyright. Hoping for a better result, Ataol wrote to Vera Kundera, who was then working as her husband's literary agent. In her initial reply, Ms. Kundera referenced a prior experience, a bad translation, someone taking liberties with the text, and said she would no longer give the rights to publish any of Mr. Kundera's work in Albanian.

Ataol wrote back to say he understood her concerns with giving up the rights. Incidentally, he added, she might want to know that there were already translations of her husband's work being published in the Albanian market, illegally, without rights, but that they, Pika pa sipërfaqe, would not do this. Here Ataol referred to Kundera's work on the problems of translation (Kundera 1996, 97–117), saying he and Arlind shared the writer's feelings on the subject. Ataol closed his message to Ms. Kundera saying he respected her decision, thanking her again for her mail, and all the best. Ms. Kundera wrote back. She had changed her mind.

This correspondence coincided with the time when the management of the copyright was passing to the Wylie Agency, so Ms. Kundera said Ataol should write to Wylie and say she sent him. Wylie responded with a questionnaire. Why do you want to publish Kundera? Why this work in particular? Why these essays rather than one of the novels? What other books have you published?

On the strength of Ataol's responses, Pika pa sipërfaqe got the rights to publish Gjini's complete translation of *Testaments Betrayed*. Seeing how this correspondence unfolded—and how easily it could have gone differently—helped me appreciate a broader takeaway that I want to briefly point out: Were it not for the young publishers' careful reading and critical understanding of Kundera's essays, it is unlikely that this intertextual map of "the novel as a modern form" would now be able to reach a new readership in Albanian. As it stands, Albanian readers can now find, in the opening pages of the text, how Kundera connects Rabelais to Rushdie (1996, 4). Or in the middle, where he argues (through Hemingway, Joyce, and other modern stylists) that capturing "the concreteness of the present has been one of the continuing trends that, since Flaubert, was to mark the evolution of the novel" (1996, 129). Or, indeed, in the last chapter, where Kundera introduces Witold Gombrowicz as the author of *Ferdydurke*, "an ingenious work barely known in Poland, totally unknown elsewhere" (1996, 248–49).

Responding to the invitation implied in Kundera's sentence, Pika pa sipërfaqe went on to publish the Polish writer's *Guide to Philosophy in Six Hours and Fifteen Minutes* (2012), *Ferdydurke* (2014), and the complete *Diary* (2019), all translated from the original by Edlira Lloha. Also conducting outward from *Testaments Betrayed* were translations of the Austrian writer Robert Musil's debut novel, *The Confusions of Young Törless* (trans. Jonila Godole, 2012), a collection titled *Ordinary and Extraordinary Stories* (trans. Bajram Karabolli, 2017) by Carlos Fuentes of Mexico, and Bruno Schulz's 1934 collection of interlinked fictions, *The Street of Crocodiles and Other Stories* (trans. Romeo Çollaku, 2018).

Each of these works opens onto a dense web of further associations. Consider, for instance, the metafictional link between Schulz's art and his real life. Before the appearance of *The Street of Crocodiles*, nothing from Schulz's literary work was available in Albanian. And while Arlind and Ataol first discovered him through Kundera, they came back to him through another route, in Bolaño. More specifically, in the climax of his 1996 novel, *Distant Star*, Bolaño describes a night with "an ideal sky" in which the narrator, Arturo B., waits anxiously in a bar, "trying to merge into the pages" of *The Complete Fictions of Bruno Schulz*:

> But Bruno Schulz's words had momentarily taken on a monstrous character that was almost intolerable. I felt that Weider's lifeless eyes were

scrutinizing me, while the letters on the pages I was turning (perhaps too quickly) were no longer beetles but eyes, the eyes of Bruno Schulz, opening and closing, over and over, eyes pale as the sky, shining like the surface of the sea, opening, blinking, again and again, in the midst of total darkness. (Bolaño 2004, 144)

Bolaño doesn't say which story his narrator—an exiled writer returned to Chile to help identify the suspected neo-fascist murderer, Weider—was trying to read. But to my mind it had to be "The Comet" (the last entry in *The Street of Crocodiles*). In the story, set in an unnamed provincial city during the time of the Second Polish Republic, Schulz combines elements of the everyday and the fantastic to show how products of imagination can wreak havoc in reality. Before the appearance of the eponymous comet,

The days passed, the hours grew longer: there was nothing to do in them. [And after . . .] Something festive had entered our lives, an eager enthusiasm. . . . [But even as] all eyes looked to the sky [awaiting] the impending end of the world [the approaching cataclysm was outpaced by] the fashion of the times [and the comet] wilted quietly amid universal indifference. (Schulz [1934] 1977, 151–59)

That Schulz was shot and killed, in 1942, by a Gestapo officer in Nazi-occupied Drogobych adds considerable gravitas to his surrealist anticipation of the thesis that the imagination and equipment of industrial modernity made it possible both to conceive and to carry out the Holocaust. Here the trail of associations connects not only with the sensibilities of repressed and exiled novelists like Kundera, Gombrowicz, and Bolaño but also with the sociological and philosophical perspectives of writers such as Zygmunt Bauman and Hannah Arendt, who translated Schulz's blinking eyes into book-length arguments that can also now be found in Pika pa sipërfaqe's catalogue.[17]

Between an Open Book and an Unwritten Future

The examples I have drawn so far indicate the range of ideas and converging relationships that connect books and people. In the still expanding list of related translations that issued outward from the excerpt of *Testaments*

Betrayed Arlind first read in *Aleph*, there are now countless other routes for other readers to trace. In 2019, to give just one more example, at a meeting in Kamëz, I spoke with community organizer Diana Malaj about her work for the grassroots organization ATA.[18] Upon entering Diana's office, I noticed an open copy of *Modernity and the Holocaust*, translated by Enis Sulstarova for Pika pa sipërfaqe in 2015. Seeing how the book was propped open in front of her computer, I asked Diana if she was using it for something she was working on.

"I am just back from Poland," she said. "We went for a seminar of remembrance and reconciliation. We visited the Gross-Rosen concentration camps. . . . I decided my first duty on return was to go back to that book. 'That's the first thing you're going to do when you go back to Kamëz,' I told myself. 'You're going to open that book.' The camps were a product of modernity, and they might happen again. We have a moral duty—"

Diana paused, collecting her thoughts before she continued. "I had a little free time," she said. "I just came from work. I was preparing the screening for the youngsters. But I am planning to write an article, and this will help me."[19]

Diana's example comes very close to what I think Arlind and Ataol meant when they said they viewed their work in publishing as something that "can help people."[20] It also illustrates why the meanings I am after in this account are not just those that inhere in the contents of books but also those that are located in the points of intersection that connect people like Arlind and Ataol—through Kundera and Gjini, Schulz and Çollaku, Bauman and Sulstarova—to the youth in Tirana and Kamëz whose futures may yet be shaped by the article Diana was writing. What those youngsters might do with the ideas that have passed through the books published by Pika pa sipërfaqe remains to be seen. In the meantime, I am content to keep shuttling back and forth, like Diana, between an open book and an unwritten future.

In the Public Interest

I, doni Gjoni, son of Bdek Buzuku . . . wished for the sake of our people to attempt, as far as I was able, to enlighten the minds of those who understand.

— GJON BUZUKU, *Missal*

On my last full day of fieldwork in 2019, I asked Arlind and Ataol to tell me what publishing meant to them. "Let's put it like this," Ataol said. "When we started this thing, we were not trying to do anything in particular other than keep reading. We just wanted to keep in contact with good books. And publishing those books came as a consequence of that. It's a very simple, maybe childish idea, if you like. If you're on a trip with a friend and you find something nice, the first thing you do is you call your friend, 'Hey, come here, look what I found!' This could describe what we were trying to do with publication. We read something really nice, and it seemed logical to try and show this nice thing. This is what publishing is to me."

"To share," Arlind added.

"It has some other connotations," Ataol continued. "It's a complicated activity, and it has some more important consequences than just showing something nice to someone, but the basic idea is in parallel to that."[1]

I return in Chapter 5 to some of the more important and complicated consequences Ataol just alluded to. But for now, following in the footsteps of Renato Rosaldo's efforts "to show the force of a simple statement taken literally" (1989, 2), I want to dwell on "the basic idea" the publishers just expressed. Arlind and Ataol put the meanings and values they attached to their publishing work to me in clear and direct terms. Reading and sharing, they said, went together in a self-evident manner. As Rosaldo might say, "Either you understand it, or you don't" (1989, 1–2).

Rather than seeking to reveal some hidden truth buried beneath the surface of their words, which speak for themselves, my goal in this chapter is to show how the publisher's unique and particular views compared to other conceptions of publishing I was able to locate within the *longue durée* of Albanian modernity. Reading my fieldnotes together with texts from Albania's national awakening in the nineteenth century and its twentieth century socialist realism, I noticed certain recurring themes that suggested I was in the presence of structures of feeling—that is, perspectives and ways of sense-making located at the intersection of my interlocutors' feelings about the past and their ideas of the future.

My general argument is as follows. Arlind and Ataol experienced everyday life in Tirana as a constant confrontation with stress, violence, and abuse of power. They saw this experience in relation to the damage done to the social fabric of the national community during the half century of a harsh dictatorship, when the state controlled virtually every aspect of public life, including the fields of literary and artistic production. Importantly, however, theirs was not only a negative view. For if the assimilation of literature authorized by an oppressive state had the power to perpetuate social problems long after the fall of the regime, it also made sense to think that a different kind of literature could help institute a new value system for an Albania yet to come. By unpacking the structures, meanings, and relationships supporting this proposition, my aim here is not to draw a single straight line connecting the past, present, and future of Albanian literary production but to show how two historically situated individuals viewed their own literary enterprise.

Structures of Feeling

In his 1973 book, *The Country and the City*, Raymond Williams used examples from English writing to trace changing attitudes toward urban and rural life in Britain and its colonies. But rather than viewing his examples just as lines in a play, passages in a novel, or verses in a poem, he saw them as structures of feeling that shaped readers' images of the past, organized their value systems in the present, and fed their visions of possible futures. Starting from a similar perspective, I use examples from a variety of Albanian sources to describe and analyze structures of feeling in the field of Albanian literary production. The sources I draw on include the colophon of a 1555 missal, the preface of an 1845 primer, the argument of an 1899 manifesto, and the closing remarks of a 1965 plenum. The bulk of the material I discuss, however, is drawn from the long conversation I opened with Arlind and Ataol in 2015.[2]

The broader goal of that long conversation has been to understand how my interlocutors saw their world and the place of books within it. My immediate goal, in this chapter, is to connect some of what I learned through immersion in their lives to a genealogy that runs through several distinct episodes from the history of Albanian literature. To clearly state now my interpretation of their interpretation: It is my view that Arlind and Ataol saw their related practices of reading, translation, and publishing as ways to exceed the limits of their given conditions, to produce new ways of thinking, and to create new realities.[3]

In the Beginning Was Translation

It was no accident that Arlind and Ataol rendered the tragedy of Albania in terms that overlapped (albeit in a structurally inverted form) with Milan Kundera's (1984) thesis in "The Tragedy of Central Europe." As we have seen, Pika pa sipërfaqe has already published translations of Kundera and many of his literary heroes. Among them, Witold Gombrowicz emerged as a favorite among readers I met in Tirana. In 2018, for example, I attended a public lecture billed as "*Ferdydurke-interpretime kritike*—a critical lecture on Witold Grombowicz's novel 'Ferdydurke,' brought to Albania by 'Pika pa sipërfaqe.'" In the talk, Klodi Leka, then a twenty-four-year-old activist studying law in Tirana, had the room rolling with laughter as he read out a passage in which an unnamed teacher begged his pupils to submit to his circular logic:

> A great poet! Remember that, it's important! And why do we love him? Because he was a great poet. A great poet indeed! . . . we love Juliuisz Słowacki and admire his poetry because he was a great poet. (2000, 42; 2014, 62)

The passage is absurd in any language. But behind the absurdist humor, I detected in the audience that evening a heightened sense of identification with the defiant student Gałkiewicz (rendered Dybeku in the Albanian translation). Dybeku's flat refusal, *"nuk mundem, nuk mundem"* (I can't, I can't) brings the pleading, sweating teacher to "a terrible impasse."

> Any moment there could be an outbreak of—of what?—of inability, at any moment a wild roar of not wanting to could erupt and reach the headmaster and the inspector, at any moment the building could collapse and bury his child under the rubble. (Gombrowicz 2000, 43–44; 2014, 63–64)

What was it in the sketch Gombrowicz penned in Warsaw around 1937 that the Tirana youth at Leka's talk in 2018 recognized as true to their experience? My sense is that it was a recognition of the absurdity—and fragility—of the totalitarian mindset that has stubbornly persisted in many sectors of Albanian public life. It was, to extrapolate further, a feeling about real people—like many of the parents of the youth at Leka's talk—who believed, who supported, who were manipulated by the state ideology, and who did not know what to do when communism fell.

Though I hesitate to generalize the sentiments of the audience in this way, my translation of their translation was not something I brought with me to the field. Rather, it was mediated by—and is in fact a paraphrase of—something Arlind said to me one afternoon as we waited out the rain under the portico of the Palace of Culture, built on the site of Tirana's old Bazaar, facing the temporary concert scaffolding emblazoned with ALBtelecom and other corporate sponsors' vision of a then-cluttered Skanderbeg square.

"They've ruined the city," Arlind said. (I recalled Ataol making a similar comment the day before. "It's not a city anymore," he said as we stepped over the ubiquitous hazards of broken pavement.) "There was something very wrong about conditions under communism," Arlind continued. "But rather than correcting that course after the nineties, it was *la même chose*, the same mistakes, the same problems, repeating under a different economic system."[4]

This notion of repeating old patterns of violence in the name of progress speaks to a much broader mentality of "modernization at any cost" that has had terrible planetary consequences—not just in Tirana. But walking in Tirana the general pattern of cutting off rather than cultivating, of censoring rather than listening, often came into sharp relief. One after-noon in summer 2019, for instance, when most everyone else was inside, keeping cool, I went out alone in the heat for a walk along Buleveradi i Ri, the New Boulevard. It was a work in progress. The completed por-tion stretched one and a half kilometers to the north from a site still called *trenit*, short for *stacioni i trenit*, or train station, though the station itself was demolished in 2013, to make room for the New Boulevard.

It was my understanding at the time that the New Boulevard would eventually connect Tirana's center to "the informal areas" in its northern periphery, including Kamëz, which were built by the communities who migrated to the capital in large numbers after the 1990s. A wide boulevard, reminiscent of the urban plans of the 1930s, in 2019 it accommodated six lanes of vehicle traffic with dedicated bike lines, pedestrian areas, play-grounds, and green spaces running along both sides. The current design was part of an ambitious and controversial urban development project re-imagined and re-launched by Erion Veliaj, who has been the mayor of Tirana since 2015, when he first ran for the office and was elected as the Socialist Party (PS) candidate.[5]

Beneath the glossy posters showing the plans for a more modern Tirana, a stenciled graffiti slogan caught my eye. It read, "*Tre parti, një oli-garki*" (Three parties, one oligarchy). Pictured above the phrase were three photo-to-stencil silhouettes showing the likeness of Edi Rama (Prime Min-ister and Chair of the Socialist Party of Albania), Lulsim Basha (leader of the opposition Democratic Party, PD), and Monika Kryemadhi (leader of the Socialist Movement for Integrity, LSI, which broke from the PS in 2004). When I passed by a few days later I saw that the likenesses and the slogan had been painted over, censored by the municipality.

After Veliaj graduated from Sami Frashëri High School in Tirana, he went on to complete degrees in the United States and the United King-dom. According to a statement reported in the British press, Veliaj sees his mandate as bringing Tirana out of a chaotic past and into a better future.

> Tirana is a great, vibrant city which nevertheless has struggled with the transition from being the centre of an isolated regime to the cosmopolitan cultural capital of the Balkans. We want to help it through the final stages of its transition and to make up for lost time. . . . Me and my team made our choice the day we took that flight back home: modernise this place at any cost. (Burgen 2018)

The Romantic Model

One of the forerunners of the Albanian Rilindja movement was the writer and activist Naum Veqilharxhi (1797–1846). Embracing the idea of Albania as a nation, Veqilharxhi opposed the division of Albanian schools along religious and linguistic lines. In his view, Albanians had not been able to form a national consciousness because rather than using Albanian as the medium of education, the communities classified as Muslim used Turkish, the Orthodox used Greek, and the Catholic used Latin or Italian. Believing Albania's cultural and political development depended on the creation of an alphabet suited to writing in Albanian, Veqilharxhi began working on an alphabet of his own invention in 1824. The result of this work, *A Very Short and Useful Primer*, was a small book written in Tosk (the southern Albanian dialect) and published in 1844. In the preface of the second edition, Veqilharxhi wrote:

> Why should it be that we, Albanians, are standing apart . . . so deprived of writing and reading in our language? . . . We can learn properly and work well enough. But only some of us are lucky enough to profit from this, while many others live in a darkness that falls heavily upon them. . . . Such considerations, my dear boys, have prompted me to take up this task without fear of the weariness I knew it would bring, not with an appetite for fame but with a feeling of duty towards my country and my mother tongue. (Veqilharxhi 2013, 260–61)

Veqilharxhi's words echo Buzuku, writer of the first Albanian book, who wished, "for the sake of our people" (as we saw in the epigraph to this chapter) "to enlighten the minds of those who understand" (Elsie 1995, 47). Like Buzuku, Veqilharxhi speaks of his labor as a duty, carried out not for personal profit but to create durable benefits for a societal "we." In this, Veqilharxhi's intimate address also resonates in some respects with the socially minded vision I would hear articulated by the cofounders of Pika pa sipërfaqe.

A related structure of feeling that reaches back to the time of the national awakening appears as a critique of the present which is set against nostalgic visions of the past. Located sometime between a writer or speaker's memories of childhood and ancient times, these visions recall the problem of perspective that Williams outlined in the context of British history

(1973, 9–12). In published works and in statements I recorded as fieldnotes, I found certain analogues to English formulas such as "Oh, happy Eden," "organic community," and "Old England." Consider, for instance, the tone and substance of the following example from Pashko Vasa (1825–1892). In his 1879 book *The Truth on Albania and Albanians*, Vasa wrote,

> Up to the period mentioned [that is, until 1831, when Vasa was six years old], the condition of Albania was brilliant. . . . Unfortunately, the change in the governmental system . . . brought disorder to the public mind. Deprived of its ancient forms by successive governors, Albania found itself the butt of the most corrupt covetousness, of innovations without consistency, of acts without cohesion. Thereby the minds of people have been troubled—torn between the recollection of the past, astonishment at the present, and uncertainty as to the future. (Vasa [1879] 2013, 124)

Between Vasa's statement and ones I heard in conversations in Tirana, there were clear differences. The main one was that my contemporary interlocutors were far less inclined to speak of a golden age. They would likely scoff if you asked them when the country was brilliant, rich, happy, and powerful. But substitute neoliberal governmentality and state capture for Ottoman domination and their picture of public confusion and disorder remained intact.

A similar vision animated the political writings of Sami Frashëri (1850–1904). Several themes from his manifesto *Albania, What Was It, What Is It, and What Will It Be?* (1899) recurred in changed but recognizable forms in the notes from my fieldwork in Tirana. What Albania was and is, according to Frashëri's account, recalled Vasa: "Albania was once a rich and prosperous country. This is no more the case" (2013, 303). From a romanticized narration of Albania's history and a sharp critique of its present condition, Frashëri went on to construct a detailed plan for moving Albania toward self-determination. The following excerpts are instructive.

> Albanians speak one of the oldest and most beautiful languages in the world. . . . How was it possible that the Albanian language survived without changes or damage despite the lack of letters, writing, and schools, while other languages written and used with great care have changed and deteriorated so much that they are now known as other languages? The answer to all these questions is very simple: Albanians preserved their lan-

guage and their nationality not because they had letters, or knowledge, or civilization, but because they had freedom, because they always stood apart and did not mix with other people or let foreigners live among them. This isolation from the world, from knowledge, civilization and trade, in one word, this savage mountain life allowed the Albanians to preserve language and nationality. (Frashëri 2013)

There can be no Albania without Albanians; there can be no Albanians without the Albanian language; and there can be no Albanian language without a writing system for it and schools in which to teach it. Therefore, language is the first thing. The Turkish government must be compelled to rescind the ban which it has imposed upon the Albanian language. It must allow Albanian schools to be opened and must let books and periodicals in Albanian enter the country unimpeded. Every Albanian must learn to read and write in Albanian, and then must learn other languages. (Frashëri 2019)

It is interesting to reflect on Frashëri's notion of isolation in light of the history of continuous migrations in this area (Vullnetari 2021). Indeed, in setting up the juxtaposition of freedom and isolation—of preserving "the oldest and most beautiful language" and of living a "savage mountain life"—it would seem that Frashëri was playing at myth making on both sides of the equation. (He himself not only migrated from his native village in southern Albania to establish a professional life in Istanbul but also worked for a time in Tripoli.) Introducing the fictive character of isolation in this context is even more curious given the recommendation of the second passage, which suggests that the preservation of the Albanian language and nationality, which once apparently depended on isolation, now required the opposite—an education that would allow Albanians to bring the knowledge of the world into Albanian language and literature. And though this was not something Frashëri could have foreseen, it was in fact from translations of Marx, Engels, Lenin, and Stalin in the 1930s that a new Albanian society would be born.

The Stalinist Model

Albania emerged from World War II under the leadership of an inexperienced communist party. Drawing on the model of Soviet socialist realism, the Party made literature an important focus of a totalizing program of social, political, and economic transformation. According to Arshi Pipa, who spent ten years (1946–1956) in an Albanian prison before escaping to Yugoslavia and migrating to the United States, Albanian literature between 1944 and 1990, "came to be the main channel for the distribution of Marxism-Leninism, through poems which were versified elaborations of party slogans and with novels fleshing out Stalin's formula that writers were the 'engineers of the human soul'" (1991, iii).

The Party, Pipa wrote, "wanted Albanian literature sifted, eliminating the darnel from the grain. The darnel included the coryphaei of Albanian literature, people such as Fishta, Noli, Schiro, Konitza, Lumo Skendó, Nikaj, Prendushi, Koliqi" (1991, 18). Cutting these thinkers out of the important work of building a new society was particularly damaging because Albania at that time, again according to Pipa, "did not have many intellectuals" (1991, 22).[6] Of the Prime Minister, Pipa wrote, "[Enver] Hoxha's level of culture was such that he did not know that the classics of Marxism occupied themselves with theoretical rather than technical problems of economy" (1991, 22). The basis for this assessment came from Hoxha himself, who justified his decision against equalizing the Albanian and Yugoslav currencies by noting, "I completed a real course for the 'intensive assimilation' of economy. For whole days and nights I read that literature from Marx, Engels, Lenin and Stalin that I could get a hold of in French, which dealt with the problems of economy" (Hoxha 1982, 317, cited in Pipa 1991, 22).

Compared to the lack of economic expertise in the upper administration, the initial situation in the literary field was considerably better. I say "initial situation" because many established writers did not survive the early years of the socialist era: "Nine writers (seven of them Catholic clergy) were shot, five died in prison, and nineteen served prison sentences" (Pipa 1991, 22). Some twenty years later, in 1965, Enver Hoxha delivered the closing remarks of the 15th Plenum of the Central Committee of the Party of Labor of Albania. In a lengthy speech titled, "Literature and Art Should Serve to Temper People with Class Consciousness for the Construction of Socialism," the Party boss laid down a set of rules and expectations for developing Albanian cultural production from a "Marxist-Leninist angle."

The title of the speech provides an adequate summary of the overall message. Starting from the idea that the collective morality of a people was variable and changeable, that it could be improved or degraded, made stronger or weaker, the Party's task, Hoxha said, was to develop a new literature and art that would strengthen and improve the consciousness of the people. The objective of literature and art, in short, was to prepare the people to accept the values and morality that were the prerequisite for "a better, more bountiful and more beautiful life and future" (Hoxha 1980, 836). Before commencing any work, writers and poets were to ask themselves, "Does this thing I am doing serve the great cause of the people?" (1980, 854).

The great cause! Remember that, it's important! Like the schoolteacher we met from *Ferdydurke*, Hoxha insisted that writers and artists should love and admire the proletarian morality of the working class because the proletarian morality of the working class was great. But for every Dybeku who refused, many more would accept the charge and would extoll in prose and poetry the new national virtues of independent life, perseverance, and social progress.

The Postsocialist Model

In June 2018, I walked down Rr. Qemal Stafa to meet Arlind. I went a little out of my way to avoid the torn-up road that ran past his office and entered the outdoor seating area of a nondescript (and unnamed) café off of Rr. Barrikadave—the Barricade Road. It was ten minutes to ten, and I was about to sit at an open table when Orges, Arlind's brother (also a bookseller), called my name. He was having a coffee with Elvis Hoxha, a writer and translator who studied philosophy in France and was now based in Tirana. I sat with them. We were joined a moment later by Enis Sulstarova, a lecturer in sociology at the University of Tirana who studied political science in Turkey, and Enis's daughter, then eight years old, who brought a copy of *Harry Potter* in translation. Arlind was last to arrive.

What turned into a good opportunity for fieldwork came about because Arlind had double-booked a meeting with me and two of his authors/translators. I was happy to postpone that day's lesson in Albanian language and literature for the chance to see how Arlind conducted his regular business. The reason for meeting with Elvis concerned a translation of Alan Badiou's hypertranslation of Plato's *Republic*, which Pika pa Sipërfaqe was interested in publishing. The business with Enis concerned a re-publication (a rarity in their catalogue) of *Democracy and Totalitarianism* by Claude Lefort, which was first translated into Albanian by the French-Kosovar philosopher Muhamedin Kullashi and published in 1993 by Shtëpia Botuese Arbri, whose copyright, if I understood correctly, was soon to expire.[7]

After concluding their business, Arlind, Enis, and Elvis shifted into casual discussion. (By then Orges had left; Enis's daughter remained content reading *Harry Potter*.) Although I listened with attention, some of their conversation eluded my understanding. When the topic of Arlind teaching me Albanian came up, for instance, I was not sure if they were simply noting this as a fact or lightly making fun of the enterprise. My uncertainty must have shown because Enis broke in just then, in English, saying, "We are discussing language, so it's very complicated."

Arlind clarified, "The philosophy of language."

"*Ska problem* [no problem]," I said. "*Vazhdo* [go on]." Their conversation from here went into literature. They talked for some time about a recent book on Migjeni (1911–1938), the Albanian poet from Shkodër who published mainly in Albanian periodicals from 1933 to his premature death in 1938. When the name of Arshi Pipa (1920–1997) came up, I interjected. I had a quote in my notebook I wanted to read out: "Our inquiry has shown so far that Albanian literature is inseparable from Albanian politics and that a study of the former amounts to a sociological study of the various manifestations of Albanian nationalism" (1978, 195).

"Okay," Elvis said. "But it's nothing special. It's a general statement. And it's normal." In other words, "It goes without saying." Or, "Isn't that true of any national literature? Isn't it true, for example, if we were speaking of French, or Russian, or Indonesian literature?" (Elvis did not actually say these "other words" but this is what he seemed to imply.)

Enis responded by affirming the statement. "Yes," he said, "historically, this is true. It's valid. The emergence of Albanian nationalism was explicitly bound up with the emergence of the written language. The literature was a functional literature. It was not an accidental or an organic connection, as might be said with Anderson's [1991] *Imagined Communities*. It was engineered. The Congress of Monastir. The establishment of the written language. The teaching of the language in Albanian schools. The first major works of literature. These all intended to establish the idea of Albania as a nation. There was an explicit political purpose in all of this. The purpose was to create and affirm the nation and national consciousness."

Elvis debated some of these points. He was making a kind of philosophical argument, talking about the universal, the singular, and a contradiction.

I had some trouble following his argument but understood it to be related to a reference Enis made to Pascale Casanova's (2004) model of literature divided into major (world) and minor (national) traditions. According to this division, Enis said, an author like Ismail Kadare would be seen as a national (that is, minor) writer, whereas Jorge Luis Borges was a major writer, concerned with humanity in global terms.

Here I interjected again. "If Kadare is an author of the national scale," I said, "are there any Albanian authors you would put on the world scale?"

"We don't have novelists of world literature status," Arlind said, "but poets, we have." Arlind named Martin Camaj (1925–1993) as one who had "something to give to the experience of Europe." He likewise recommended Mitrush Kuteli (1907–1967). Also mentioned (though by whom is not clear from my notes) were Petro Marko (1913–1991), Kasëm Trebeshina (1926–2017), and Agron Tufa (b. 1967).

When I asked about one of the Albanian novelists recently published by Pika pa sipërfaqe, Elvis looked away with a gesture that said, "hm, I don't know about that." He then said, "We have writers but not literature." After a brief pause, again moving from the particular to the universal, he extended the "we" beyond the nation, saying, "That's the problem in the world today."

Structures of Feeling Revisited

From conversations such as the ones reported in this chapter, I built up a picture of my interlocutors' vision of publishing as a public service that was at odds with the harsh realities they experienced in everyday life. To keep that picture grounded in verbatim statements about how Arlind and Ataol saw things, I arranged in late summer 2019 to record a conversational interview in their office near Sami Frashëri High School in Tirana. The discussion that follows moves chronologically through an edited version of that interview, the full transcript of which came to a little more than 10,000 words. A few days before recording the interview, I explained in separate meetings with Arlind and Ataol what I had in mind. I told them I wanted to try to pin down why they used three specific words in the short description they posted on their publishing house's official website.[8] The words were *i pavarur* (which in English would be the equivalent of "independent"); *jofitimprurës* (which translates as "nonprofit"); and *social* (which is pronounced differently in Albanian but has the same broad and multivalent connotations as the English word derived from the same Latin roots).[9]

It was apparent to me by then that the meanings of these common Albanian adjectives diverged in certain respects from my concepts. For example, when I thought of an independent publisher, I thought of a small press that had not been subsumed by a big publishing group. But since there were no big publishing groups in Albania, saying Pika pa sipërfaqe was *i pavarur* had to convey something else. Wanting to know what that something else was, I opened the conversation by asking, "Do you think it might be misleading for me, when writing about your project, to translate *i pavarur* as independent?"[10]

"The Albanian term has some similarities with the original term in English," Ataol said. "But there are some important differences. I know something of what 'independent publisher' means abroad, which is basically 'not connected to some business conglomerate.' This is not the case here. . . . To me, *i pavarur* has more political connotations, meaning we are independent from any political party or any other state or public institution."

"He wrote that [description for the website]," Arlind said, referring to Ataol. "But for me, it's not a problem."

"But does being *i pavarur*," I replied to Arlind, "have some kind of—"

"Reality?" Arlind said. "This is difficult to say. We are dependent on our collaborators and our public and many others who support us. Our families. Our funders. So, we are *dependent*. But I think what Ataol is saying is that we are *open*. We don't have an ideology, a program, or a political agenda. We are independent insofar as we don't have a 'hidden side.' Otherwise, we are dependent. Very, very dependent. Because our families support us, our friends, collaborators, you, the public."

Arlind paused, considering his words. "Maybe here," he continued, "*i pavarur* has more significance than 'independent' does abroad because, here, after the nineties, the modern publishing houses were created by people who were dependent on the old communist regime. . . . So this is one reason. The second is that the people with the ability to go into publishing in the nineties were privileged, from the state."

"They had political affiliations," Ataol said. "Or were family members of someone with political power."

"This was the context I think Ataol had in mind," Arlind said. "And he chose that word to distinguish from this."

"This is fairly correct," Ataol said.

Though I now had a better grasp of the specific connotations *i pavarur* had for the publishers, I was still not sure whether Arlind and Ataol thought the connotations they attached to the term were likely to be shared by other members of the Albanian reading public. So I asked, "Do you think the word has a positive connotation for your readers?"

Ataol began his response by reminding me of some basic facts and perspectives that, although quite important, were sometimes easy for me to lose sight of. "We do at best 500-copy print runs," he said. "300 in many cases. And even those print runs take at least two or three years to run out. Sometimes four, five years. So we're talking about a really small public. But even though the number is very small, I wouldn't feel comfortable in putting all these readers in the same box. Saying 'our readers.' That's a very broad generalization."

I appreciated Ataol's refusal to generalize, not least because it kept me honest about my own commitments to writing "ethnographies of the particular" (Abu-Lughod 1991). I also appreciated that after establishing these limitations, Ataol went on to answer my question.

"For these readers," he said, "small number though they might be, I don't think this word 'independent' has ever played any role in their interpretation of our work. If you ask, I'm pretty sure, no one will refer to us as an independent publisher. And by independent I'm using the Albanian conception [*i pavarur*]."

"For some groups here," Arlind said, "we seem like Communists. For some actual Communists, we seem like Liberals. For some religious groups, we seem like agnostics. But I think they feel something very near to that word. During our contacts with our readers, I feel that they perceive us as people who are not connected directly with the establishment."

After an exchange of anecdotes that gave me a very clear image of the kind of readers that appreciated the work they were doing, I steered the conversation back to the topic of cultural translation. "I want to return," I said, "to the meaning of the phrase, 'conceived as a social, nonprofit project.'"

"Well," Ataol said, "we wouldn't necessarily mind being able to have, by Albanian standards, two good salaries on which to live and keep doing what we're doing. But in the last ten, eleven years, this has not been possible. . . . Again, we might have diverging opinions, me and Arlind, but I wouldn't want this to turn into a profitable business because then, I think, at a certain point along the way we would lose control over our ideas concerning publication, why we started it, and why we're doing it."

"Profit is not our goal," Arlind said.

"We're doing what we're doing," Ataol continued, "because we like books. . . . That was what I meant when I stated, 'it was conceived from the beginning as a social project.' I meant that it was not meant to be profitable but to benefit society."

"Publishing is not a conventional business," Arlind said. "It concerns a product of the mind. It helps people. It is done in the public interest. Publishing is—"

"But there are profitable presses," Ataol said.

"Okay," Arlind acknowledged, "but the point is that publishing is in the public interest. Books are not like other products or commodities. They're another thing."

That publishing was not a conventional business, that it was supposed to help people, and that books were not like other products—these were all very important ideas to pursue, I thought. But before I could put together a proper follow-up, Ataol continued from where Arlind left off.

"I know of conceptions of profit as benefiting society," Ataol said. "But personally, I don't see individual profit as a contribution, at least not in publishing. It's probably a bad establisher of value. If you want to formulate a set of criteria that will measure what you're doing in terms of, 'Is it in the benefit of society or not?' I don't think profit would rank among those criteria. I'm not sure they're directly related, like one can be the consequence of the other, or they're just two foundational ideas, but if you want to try to formulate what we are, those two probably stand together. We're both a socially minded activity and a not-for-profit organization."

"But 'social project' does not mean we are just socialists," Arlind said. "Publishing is a public activity, to spread knowledge. It's one of the means to emancipate society. This is why this is a social project."

I want to interrupt the flow of the conversation here to make a few methodological remarks. As I indicated in the introduction, I do not see my job as an ethnographer to be just like that of a reporter preparing a fact-checked profile. Rather, the work of ethnography is, in my view, about generating intersubjective knowledge through long-term immersion in people's lives. To make these statements more concrete, I think it would be helpful here to compare the present account with a question-and-answer interview titled "Albania: These Independent Publishers Who Fight for the Distribution of Books and Literature," published by the French journalist Louis Seiller in 2017.

As a kind of triangulation or verification, Seiller's piece would seem to corroborate the information I obtained by similar means—that is, "by recording interviews with ordinary people and patching the results into coherent shape" (Zinsser 2006, 106). For example, reflecting that a lot has changed in Albania since the 1990s, Sellier asked Arlind and Ataol (in French), "How do you see your [for-profit] colleagues today? What makes you different from them?"

> AK: The main difference is that we read! And consistently. It is our readings that brought us to the profession. Our approach is different because, from the start, we have chosen foundational works [e.g., *The Ethics* of Spinoza]. Many of those who worked for the state simply reissued translations that already existed. They started to publish turnips because they do not have a real editorial vision.

> AN: Many publishers exist only to promote the interests of their owner. Their literary knowledge is limited. We like to share and discuss our readings. There are only two or three publishing houses [in Albania] that have this approach, and they translate Jacques Rancière or Alain Badiou. (Seiller 2017)

Seiller asked good questions, and the report he produced conveys a lot of information in a very tight package (1600 words). Not only that, but I also recognize in Arlind and Ataol's responses the same warmth and humor I came to know through immersing myself in their daily lives. And though this might just be a matter of what got left on the cutting room floor, I do however see an important difference in what came through the interview I recorded in the same office on the same topics. And I think that difference—intimate, particular, and grounded in the everyday—depended on the relationship of trust I built with Arlind and Ataol over a long period of time. This comes through, for example, in the following turn in our conversation.

"But now," Arlind said, following his clarification that their project was social, not socialist, "we're confronting new difficulties. Maybe now it's time to have more sure steps, a strategy. I'm more stressed now than I was five or ten years ago. Ten years ago we didn't know what we were doing."

"Our life quality has been in decline," Ataol said.

"Yes," Arlind said, "I think we need to change something. A new experience or new strategy, a new method. But I find this very difficult. I like our way of working, but it has consequences."

"The workload has become very difficult to manage," Ataol said. "On the one hand, the number of books in publication has been growing. We are now more than one hundred titles. On the other, we are already operating at very strained budgets. . . . The number of books keeps growing and the amount of time [we have to work] is being restricted. We both have small children."

"Everyday life in Albania is difficult," Arlind said. "It's crazy here, in Tirana."

"You have to imagine creatures living in very extreme conditions," Ataol said. "Like the animals at the bottom of the sea or those living at very high temperatures in the desert. This is the kind of existence."

"When we say, 'the power' here, 'the corruption,' all these things are bonded with our everyday life," Arlind added.

"We experience corruption," Ataol said. "We experience abuse of power, we experience violence."

"Everyday life in Albania is the key to understanding all these things," Arlind said. "Because in my everyday life, year after year, I've had a lot of difficulties, of a kind I never imagined. Never. The politicians and corrupt people here have colonized our everyday life with buildings, with corruption, with mafia, with all their instruments of power. Everyday life here is very, very stressful. And they say, 'The only way to improve your everyday life is to have money.' To become like them."

Conclusion: Literature's Historicity

The living social histories of Albanian publishing companies such as Onufri, Toena, Çabej, Aleph, IDK, Zenit, and Pika pa sipërfaqe remain largely untold. Outside a relatively small but transnational circle of contemporary readers, even the names are mostly unknown. From the standpoint of ethnographic storytelling (McGranahan 2020), however, I think the likes of Bujar Hudhri of Onufri, Gentian Çoçoli of Aleph, Piro Misha of IDK, and Krenar Zejno of Zenit Editions would all make excellent informants.

Drawing from my fieldwork with Arlind and Ataol, I wish to contribute to the inevitably larger project, which I hope future researchers will join me in pursuing, of doing biblio-ethnography with Albanian sources. My discussion of the ethnographic material in this chapter sought to show how my interlocutors' decisions about what and how to read, translate, and publish in the present have been structured by their past experiences and future expectations. In that regard, my argument built on and can contribute to a large body of interdisciplinary theory dealing with overlapping experiences of past and future times in the present.[II]

Ultimately, Arlind and Ataol had a social vision that was irreducibly their own. But their conception of Pika pa sipërfaqe as an independent, nonprofit, social project also resonated with earlier public projects in Albania. My analysis of the projects in question has shown that, despite very significant differences, they overlapped in three important ways. First, they all were grounded in a critique of the present. Second, they all were oriented toward a vision of a better future. And third, they all operated with an idea of literature as a means of social transformation. Evidence for these claims appears in documents authored by the intellectual leaders of the Albanian National Awakening in the nineteenth century, by the communist Party ideologues who dominated the public sphere in the second half of the twentieth century, and in statements I recorded as fieldnotes in the present of the ethnography.

Approaching these areas of overlap as structures of feeling can help explain my interlocutors' view of publishing as a social activity. For even as their conception of books took shape in a space built on the ruins of a past in which literature was made to function as a tool of totalitarian control, they saw publishing as something to be done in the public interest. Publishing, they said, was a way to emancipate readers by spreading knowledge and raising social awareness.

In their work, Arlind and Ataol operated according to a strong feeling of social responsibility. Through their publishing enterprise they enacted a politics of recuperation in Francisco Martínez's sense of "a performed valuation and valorisation, meant to affirm a collective idea through daily engagement with practices of care" (Martínez 2020, 4). Caring both about books and about the people who read them, they did not speak of literature's function in the abstract. They referred to concrete knowledge and new realities that were different from the precarious everyday life they and their readers knew all too well. And though I cannot necessarily point to a given book or a collection of books and say, "Here is a new way of thinking," or "There is a new social reality," there are clear indications that among the many books Pika pa sipërfaqe has published, some have already begun to help people—including, as we have seen, activists and community organizers such as Diana Malaj and Klodi Leka—as they go to work in their communities, trying to overcome the inertia of ambivalence and mistrust that has long permeated public life in Tirana.

4

Reading Nearby

I do not intend to speak about. Just speak nearby.

— TRINH T. MINH-HA, *Reassemblage*

In "Textual Interpretation as Collective Action," the sociologist Elizabeth Long summoned the iconographic history of the solitary reader to indicate some of the powerful but partial "lenses through which we have envisioned reading as a cultural practice" (1993, 181). Long's aim was not to deny the personal and private dimensions of reading but to call our attention to the "social infrastructure" and "social framing" that organizes and orchestrates so much of what goes into literate activity.[1] Education scholar Marilyn Cochran-Smith's 1984 monograph, *The Making of a Reader*, provided a case in point. Believing that to talk about reading in a meaningful way, "it is necessary to understand its meaning for participants," Cochran-Smith used the methods of ethnography "to peel away the layers of context into which [her subjects' reading was] embedded" (Cochran-Smith 1984, 37).[2] What she found was that the children in the study community learned how to "use and understand the written word" long before acquiring the "mechanical skills of encoding and decoding print" (Cochran-Smith 1984, 2). In other words, "the making of readers in this community was the process of gradual socialization, rather than direct teaching" (Cochran-Smith 1984, 2). This finding, which unsettled the received wisdom from decades of decontextualized cognition and comprehension studies, is indicative of what the tools of ethnography can contribute to the social analysis of reading.

In what follows I apply the perspective exemplified by Cochran-Smith's study to the ethnography of the literary community attached to Pika pa sipërfaqe. I approach participants' reading practices, in Long's (1993) terms, as a form of "collective action." While the ethnography of reading I perform here still does not allow us to see inside the head of a solitary reader, it does make it possible to examine reading as a social practice. By foregrounding the extent to which reading takes place within social relationships and is driven by social objectives, the general approach I advocate—reading nearby—can open a way to a broader analysis of the complex contexts in which literate activity occurs. In addition to providing a fuller picture of the little-known literary community at the center of the present account, then, my aim here is also to offer a flexible approach for exploring new directions in media and literary anthropology.

Making a Field

In the introduction to the 1968 collection *Literacy in Traditional Societies*, the anthropologist Jack Goody outlined a method for studying "the potentialities of literate communication" (1968a, 4). Reaching back to this method, the initial purpose of my research in Albania was to collect ethnographic material on what Goody called "the uses made of writing in a particular social setting" (4). The setting I selected was a Tirana bookshop that my partner, Smoki, also an anthropologist and a Tirana native, first introduced to me, in 2008, as "a hangout for writers." When I returned in 2015, in addition to the scene of reading I was looking for, I found a part-localized, part-dispersed, and part-imagined community composed of readers, writers, artists, and translators.

What prompted my visit on the day I met Arlind and Ataol for the first time was a post I saw on the store's Facebook page, which read, "*Panairi i Librit të Përdorur. Sot, nesër dhe pasnesër*—Used Book Fair. Today, tomorrow, and the day after." The set up for the book fair consisted of a few tables arranged in the bookstore's interior courtyard. Arlind's collection of used books, displayed in horizontal rows with the spines facing up, covered two tables. The third featured new books in pristine condition with striking cover art and authors I recognized and liked: Arendt, Borges, Calvino, Clastres, Joyce, Todorov, Vonnegut. Along with these writers' names, here is what I recorded in my notebook that day.

15 June 2015. I made it finally to my research site [E për-7-shme]. Brizi's Tardis-like description [bigger on the inside] was accurate.[3] From the outside it still looks like a small and narrow space. But turning the corner to what was once a compact interior courtyard now opens onto several additional rooms and gardens. I met two guys—young, friendly, looking much like hipsters—who are running the bookstore and a publishing house. Today was an event, a book sale. Top Channel was there, doing a feature for the evening news. The first book put out by their company was Vonnegut's *Slaughterhouse-Five*—a nice anthropological connection. They also have *Breakfast of Champions* and others. (I will list.)

The note, which I wrote by hand, goes on for another two-and-a-half pages in a US-standard "college ruled" notebook. There are descriptions of the crowd around the table where the books were displayed (lively); comments on the atmosphere and music (pleasant); doubts (about the possibility of doing ethnography); and reassurances: "Be patient."

The last part of the entry includes a description of a scene in which "the owners and their friends" were taking pictures of one another "with a film-roll camera." The note closes with a comment on that scene: "Seems fitting for a group that starts a publishing house in the digital age." If not for my notes, I'm sure I would have forgotten this detail. The oddity I registered upon first encountering young people in Tirana who valued the slower, more deliberate processes of working with analog media strikes me now as a sign of the transformation I have undergone since this project began. In a fieldnote from July 19, 2021, for example, I wrote: "We stopped in front of the Ulçin Photo shop. Arlind was dropping off a roll of film to be developed. I waited outside. He wore a mask to go in. Something almost no one here is now doing." The "something" here referred to the protective measure of mask-wearing in the middle of a pandemic. That Arlind and Ataol still have their film developed I now took for granted.

Another indicator of this transformation comes through the "indexical excess" (Taylor 1996) that remains visible in the hand-written note. That I put the umlaut on the wrong e in E për-7-shme, for example. Or that I never referred to Arlind and Ataol by name. But even before I had the names of the "two guys," we already shared a connection of value—through the books they had on display. The "nice anthropological connection" Kurt Vonnegut represented for me was a kind of ethnographic serendipity. The first thing we talked about together, after I introduced myself as a researcher with an interest in reading cultures, was how Vonnegut (and his narrator in *Slaughterhouse-Five*) studied anthropology at the University of Chicago. Looking back I can say that my relating to the young publishers' editorial choices in this way, responding favorably to seeing something of myself in their work, provided an early indication of the particular intersubjective qualities of the ethnography that would follow.

After our first conversation about Vonnegut's anthropology, I said I would like to talk with them more about their work and asked if I could have an interview. "Sure," they said, but now was very busy. I could see. Customers filed by the tables as we spoke, inquiring about the books and purchasing two, three, and four titles at a time. The meeting ended with them saying I should "come back tomorrow." When I returned the next day, and for many days after that, I found the two booksellers still very busy. Exactly one month after our first meeting, Arlind came over to the table where I sat drinking hot tea on a hot day and said, "I remember you wanted to talk." This was the opening to a series of interviews—first with Arlind, and later with Ataol—that developed into an ongoing research relationship.

The Social Practice of Reading Nearby

The first time I asked Ataol about the origins of the publishing house, he said, "My meeting with Arlind was by chance. I was looking for some authors and Arlind was working at the bookstore."[4] Through later fieldwork and writing, I came to see this chance occurrence through the lens of the intimate social practice I call "reading nearby." Through books, talk, and the exchange of ideas, the two friends, the publishing company, and the transnational community attached to it all followed in a trail of associations, from one mediator to the next. Chance was there. But Ataol's meeting with Arlind also depended on a set of specific reading and discussion practices. Without their overlapping interests in authors and books, Arlind and Ataol may still have crossed paths in the reprivatized house that became a bookstore, but that probably would have been the end of their association.

A key layer of context needed to understand what reading meant to Arlind and Ataol was their shared belief, traced in the previous chapter, that literature has the power to shape social imagination and therefore to transform social reality. As we have seen, Arlind and Ataol expressed this idea, in informal conversation and through their work, both in positive and negative terms. In its negative construction, it formed the basis for their critique of the national literature of Albanian Socialist Realism, the celebratory histories of the state, and the limited views of the outside world that came through the translations that were filtered through the state censors during communism. In positive terms, it was their reason for bringing something new to Albania's market for books. Some of their publications, like the Albanian writer Virion Graçi's *Stina e Hijeve*, *The Season of Shadows*, which the Ministry of Culture of Albania awarded the Best Literary Book of 2014, have contributed something new from within the established literary tradition. Others, such as Simone Weil's *Gravity and Grace* (trans. Blerta Hyska, 2018), came from far outside that tradition.

The style of Weil's writing, and the thoughts it conveyed, Arlind told me while he was correcting the proofs of an already edited translation, were different from other French intellectuals. "Her thought wasn't grounded in the legacy of Marx and Hegel but in a more . . . humanistic way" he said.[5]

Arlind expressed the sentiment represented by the ellipses in the text above by gesturing with his hands, from his chest, an outpouring from the heart to the reader or listener. He said he first read Weil's 1949 book *The Need for Roots*, and it was "fantastic, beautiful, but very difficult." Then he found *Gravity and Grace*. It was much more accessible, he said, "not schematic, with a short paragraph style, almost like a prose poem." He started to read out, then had me read to myself, a paragraph about a failed suicide. Since time is not real but reality depends on time, the passage suggested, our existence depends on the nonexistent. Precisely this idea, he said, would be "good for Albanian readers."

As I discuss later in this chapter, I picked up a trace the next summer—in conversation with Diana Malaj in Kamëz—of some effects *Gravity and Grace* had already had on local readers. I don't know what further outcomes, if any, may issue from the ones I registered at that time. What is certain, however, is that the many unique and particular technologies of imagination that Arlind and Ataol have put into circulation—through Pika pa sipërfaqe—have created the possibility of bringing their literary ideals into material form.

A Reader's Methods: Interpersonal and Intertextual

In my first interview with Arlind I learned that he started working with books around age fifteen, in Elbasan, where he grew up. His first job was at the bookstore owned by Pëllumb Zekthi, Rudian's brother. "Pëllumb had a beautiful bookstore in the center of Elbasan," he said. "I started to frequent this bookstore after my third year of high school, and Pëllumb offered me a job. There I had the possibility to learn more about books— literature, philosophy—and business. I also met Rudian there. He inspired me to become more knowledgeable about literature and philosophy." It was a summer job, just for three months. A year later Arlind left home to attend the University of Tirana, where he completed a degree in Albanian language and literature in 2006. Since then, he said, "I just read books."[6]

When I asked what sorts of books, he said, "We read a lot. Fiction, philosophy, poetry. The reading leads to translations, and we've published about ten books a year since 2009."[7]

"How do you decide which books to translate?" I said.

"It's very simple," he said. In fact, there were two ways. The first method was interpersonal: "If a friend tells us about a book, we'll pick it up when we get a chance and begin to read. If we like it, we'll contact a translator and make a contract to do the translation." The second method was intertextual: moving from book to book.

On the day of our first interview, Arlind explained this method using the example of Milan Kundera's *Testaments Betrayed*. You start with an author you like and respect. You then read with an eye to discovering the authors they read and respect. Kundera thus becomes like the friend with a recommendation. He tells you about a book. When you get a chance, you read it. If you like it, you contact a translator, make a contract, do the translation.

In my last period of fieldwork, in summer 2021, I came upon another example. While Arlind and Ataol were busy at work in their office, I read from their copy of the English translation of Bolaño's *Between Parentheses*. There was underlining throughout. Most of the underlining was of authors' names, or titles of works. Later, after lunch, while having a very good Turkish coffee at a café across the street from their office, I asked Ataol if he was the one doing the underlining.

"No," he said. "It was Arlind. I read the book in Albanian."[8]

They published the translation (*Në parantezë*, trans. Bashkim Shehu) in late 2019 so Ataol knew the text very well. I asked about the writer/author-ess distinction that came into the last interview I read that morning.[9] Ataol remembered that "the writer" (i.e., the artist) was Silvina Ocampo. But Arlind was the one who underlined her name.

"I completed a whole course in Latin American literature," Arlind said, laughing. "All the writers Bolaño mentions. I bought them. Studied them."

From the standpoint of biblio-ethnography, I was particularly interested to learn how the publishers' interpersonal and intertextual methods came together. The story behind the Albanian translation of *Ferdydurke* was a case in point. As we have seen, when Arlind and Ataol first learned of this "ingenious work," indirectly, through *Testaments Betrayed*, Gombrowicz was largely unknown in Albania. Because of Pika pa sipërfaqe, his writing is now available for the first time in Albanian. But for Arlind and Ataol to bring *Ferdydurke* from the original Polish into Albanian took more than simply discovering the work through Kundera or tracking it down to read in the Spanish, French, and English translations; it depended on another chance meeting—grounded in the social practice of reading nearby. This time it was with Edlira Lloha, a Tirana-born immigrant to Poland who stopped by the bookshop on a return visit to her native city.

"We started talking," Arlind said. "We had read Gombrowicz—the greatest author of all time! And she spoke Polish.[10] Now, we are collaborating on a big project to translate all Gombrowicz's works."[11]

The Ethnographic Technique of Reading Nearby

Of all the interpersonal and intertextual methods Arlind and Ataol used in their work, the most important appeared to be located within their relationship to one another. The basis of this relationship was a shared outlook on social life. This came through most clearly in their critique of what they regularly termed, "Albanian society." Though they were keenly aware of the ethics and politics of ethnographic representation, neither Arlind nor Ataol attempted to conceal from me the problems they saw in their social world.[12] "It's a mess," Arlind said characteristically. "Albanian society is riddled with corruption in all sectors. The government, the economy, the mass media, education. All sectors of power are infected."[13]

The early impressions I formed from this and similar statements of disenchantment with the social and economic transformations taking place in Albania led me to believe, incorrectly, that Arlind was expressing a kind of postsocialist nostalgia. I have since come to understand his sentiments, more accurately, within the context of the pointed "memories of communism" (not to be mistaken for nostalgic modes of remembering) that have become a powerful motif among Tirana artists and writers of his generation (Kalo 2017).

Indeed, if there was an Albanian past Arlind longed for, it was not the past of his memory or childhood experience but one from his reading and discussion of history before 1944, the year Enver Hoxha came to power. "Communism and Stalinism," he said, "were distant, ideologically and geographically. But once the country took that turn, we [Albanians] were forgotten by Europe, ignored, left behind."[14]

While I did not realize it then, these excerpts from my early conversations with Arlind contained all the elements of the ethnographic approach I now call reading nearby. I went into this research wanting to generate material about literary culture, so I asked about literary things. But the salient themes that emerged from my notes were not just Arlind's insights on reading and books but his views about "violence," "corruption," and the other "stresses of quotidian existence" in Tirana. These verbatim statements, which I jotted down during our first in-depth conversation, didn't relate directly to Arlind's reading practices. They did, however, open a window into how he viewed his social world.

Another keyword Arlind used, which functioned as a kind of verbal punctuation, was *katastrofë*, which is pronounced differently but carries the same meaning as the English word, catastrophe. For example, later in the interview quoted above, he said: "The professors at Albanian University [a for-profit university] are professors in name only. They got their position by power, or by their proximity to power. They don't read. They don't know contemporary theory. *Katastrofë*. The big publishers have corrupted these professors. They're assigning bestsellers. *Katastrofë*. There are now sixty private universities in the city. *Katastrofë*." Here Arlind made his hands into the shape of a pyramid, the suggestion being that the private universities were running a kind of Ponzi scheme—similar to the one that led to the country's spectacular financial collapse in 1997.[15]

With this talk of *katastrofë*, Arlind was opening a whole social world for me. But rather than seizing the opportunity to inquire further into his social reality, I again tried to steer the conversation to the topic of publishing. To this Arlind replied: "The book industry in Albania, like other things, is without rules. It's all black."

He then pivoted from black-market publishing to a diagnosis of Albania's first decade of post-communism—a diagnosis I later found corroborated in anthropologist Clarissa De Waal's (2014) account of this period: "In the nineties," Arlind said, "there was a global change, and communism fell. But deep down it was the same. The former elites became the current elites. Those who had power opened the publishing houses, continuing their monopoly on power and knowledge. And now, in Tirana, a city of a million people, there are more than one hundred publishing houses. *Katastrofë.*"

"But why is it bad that there are so many publishers?" I asked.

"Because," he said, "most of these publishers don't read. They're just looking to make money, or to launder money. They think, 'why not?' And they start a publishing house."

Looking for a Journal, Finding a Community

A week after my first extended interview with Arlind, I sat down with Ataol on the Turkish sofa at the back of the bookstore. Ataol said I could ask him anything. I asked if he could walk me through his relationship to the bookshop itself.

"It starts with a journal," he said.[16]

Ataol had been looking for copies of *E për-7-shme*, which the reader will remember was an avant-garde literary magazine from the 1990s that only went to four numbers. This is what prompted his first visit to the bookstore. At that time, he had just graduated with a degree in economics and gone into business importing car parts from Turkey. But he was not happy with the work. "The part I really didn't like," he said, "was dealing with customs [officers]."

This was around 2006, a time when Albania's reputation for corruption had come to the forefront of public discourse. Like Arlind, Ataol spoke of this reputation in unflinching terms: "Corruption here is endemic," he said. "All the illicit goods that are trafficked in Albania are trafficked with the complicity of customs. . . . And even though I was always trying to do everything by the book, they would always come up with something, some obscure bureaucratic regulation, and the point of it was to get a bribe. They held up a perfectly legitimate import until the bribe was given."

Ataol found the literary atmosphere at the bookstore a welcome contrast to his daytime experience. So he started spending more of his free time there, getting to know the others who did the same. And though he didn't end up finding any copies of the journal he went looking for, he managed to establish social relationships with other like-minded readers—including Arlind, who was then working evenings as the bookstore attendant. In conversation with Arlind and other regulars, Ataol learned that the shop was going bankrupt. "This was the path that opened for us. I had the financial possibility to invest, and this place closed down for three months, and we moved things around, brought in new chairs, opened up this room."

This was also when Ataol discovered Kurt Vonnegut, the author of his first translation project. "I came across a synopsis online," he said, referring to *Slaughterhouse-Five*. "It sounded like something I would like, so I ordered it. This was a time when you could do that. If I had heard of the book just a few years earlier [before Amazon shipped to Albania], it wouldn't have been possible for me to buy a copy, and I probably would have forgotten all about it."

"Was there something about the writing that made you want to translate it?" I said.

"It wasn't that the content of the novel pushed me toward anything," he said. "It was just that I thought this would be a good one to, you know, to translate into Albanian. When I started that, I didn't have any plan to do anything with the translation. It was just something I wanted to do, and I enjoyed doing it."

That Arlind was not then reading English might suggest a more concrete motive for Ataol to translate Vonnegut into Albanian: it was a way for him to share the book he was reading with his friend, so they could talk about it. Eventually, after they went through the text together line by line, correcting the translation, they contacted a mutual friend, who was not an established publisher but who "had the documentation and ability to publish." This friend did not say "no" outright, but he was not very enthusiastic about the proposal. So Arlind and Ataol talked some more. And Ataol said, "Well, he just has the documents to publish. We might as well get those documents ourselves."

The documents did not cost much—about five hundred dollars—so they went to a notary public, paid the fee, and the publishing house was born. All they needed now was permission from Vonnegut's estate to publish the copyrighted material. Even though unauthorized translations are commonplace in the Albanian market, Arlind and Ataol were determined to follow the proper legal procedures.[17] So Ataol went to the website, KurtVonnegut.com, found the contact for the author's long-time agent,

Donald Farber, and wrote an email explaining that he translated the book and would like to publish it in Albania. Farber replied with generous terms, to say the least. For $1.00, the rights were theirs.[18] When the book was printed, Ataol sent Farber three copies along with a 200 Lekë note, effectively paying double.[19]

Opening up to Moments of Transition

My research on Albanian literary culture began with an effort to generate observational data on the everyday social phenomena that the writer Georges Perec once termed "what happens when we read" (Perec 2008, 175). But unlike the method Perec outlined, which foregrounded the actions of the eyes, voice, hands, and bodily posture that made reading a "technique of the body" (Mauss 1973), the approach I adopted was to focus on the social contexts in which these actions are embedded and the social relationships conducting outward from them.

Rather than generating insights about the embodied experience of reading itself, this approach revealed the social issues that touched the lives of people who, in addition to being serious readers, were also trying to create an institution they hoped might contribute to improving conditions in a city and a country they experienced as "violent," "broken," and "riddled with corruption." So while the critique of Albanian society that emerged as my interlocutors' central concern did not relate directly to questions about literature and books, our talk of authors, ideas, publishing, and translation provided a context and a "way in" to a social world I would have been unlikely to access by other means. This is precisely what reading nearby amounts to as an ethnographic technique.

In that respect it resembles the approach Helena Wulff (2017) developed in *Rhythms of Writing: An Anthropology of Irish Literature*. In this contribution to literary anthropology (which also happens to concern a small country on the margins of Europe, albeit one that boasts a disproportionate number of writers of global renown), Wulff approaches Irish fiction as a "complex commentary of contemporary life in Ireland" (2017, 58). Her method thus conforms to the basic principle of reading nearby—that is, to take literate activity as a point of entry rather than as an object or unit of analysis.

My own adoption of this principle reaches back to my socialization within the interpretive community of visual anthropology. Inspired by filmmaker Trinh Minh-ha's (1982) notion of "speaking nearby," I approach reading, like speaking, not as a bounded event but as an activity consisting of "moments of transition opening up to other possible moments of transition" (Chen 1992, 87).[20] Rather than trying to "objectify" the act of reading, therefore, I relate to it more as a mediating object—like a lens. By shifting the emphasis from the phenomenology to the sociology of reading (Dulin 1974; Iser 1978), what reading nearby ultimately seeks to make visible are not the intellectual or emotional components of a reader's response (to a novel, for example) but the social relationships, projects, and partnerships co-produced through the meeting of like-minded readers— for example, in a Tirana bookshop.

The Ethnographic Good and the Goal of Reading Nearby

As often happens in fieldwork, what was "good" for the ethnographer was not so great for the subjects of the ethnography. In this case, the discovery of water damage in the storeroom at the bookstore presented an opportunity for me to move into a more participatory role. "You're on the staff now," Arlind joked the day after I helped with the off-site transfer of books. The day after that, over a lunch of *tavë pikant*, I got an Albanian nickname (Meti), received instruction on table manners (bread on the table, not the plate; salad direct from the bowl, not served out "like the bourgeoisie"), and began to see for myself, through many informal and unstructured details, the quiddity of a friendship rooted in a shared passion for reading. This passion was present in nearly everything Arlind and Ataol did. Books were the background, the foreground, the context, the topic, the activity, and the outcome.

Their commitment to social critique came through with a similar intensity. But rather than centering on direct action, their conversation followed a more indirect path: through literature. Each new translation project they tackled and each new book they released seemed to embody their belief that the failure of public institutions in Albania stemmed in some significant measure from a failure of imagination. The root of the problem, as I understood their view of it, was that Albanian writing had dwelled for too long in the "small context" of the nation's literary tradition. And though they were careful to not speak of relations in history in terms of cause and effect, they did draw connections between conditions during communism and conditions today, as these relate both to their experience of everyday life and their view of Albanian literature.

From taking part in their conversations, my growing sense was that their dedication to reading, translating, and publishing foundational works of literature and philosophy was driven by a desire to heal some of the wounds that were inflicted—in both literary and social spaces—by the way things were done during communism. On the one hand, they were critical of the new generation of writers and artists who still deified rather than subverted or refuted the older generation—represented most prominently by Ismail Kadare. On the other hand, they appreciated the extent to which there was also renewal, and they celebrated counterhegemonic voices such as Fatos Lubonja. But whether it was through their resistance to the continuation of the old cultural and political elite or their embrace of artists and intellectuals who represented something new, the issue that seemed most in need of addressing was captured in a phrase that recurred numerous times in my fieldnotes—that is, "the damage done by forty-five years of harsh communism."

As the exiled Albanian writer Arshi Pipa knew all too well, Albanian literature from this period was subject to the state's vision of the Stalinist doctrine and "the Albanian intellectual had no other choice than to either accept the Party line one hundred percent or else end up in jail" (1991, 21). In addition to dictating what local authors could write, the state-directed projects of cultural production in communist Albania also criminalized "the consumption of foreign media and popular culture as expressions of *shfaqe të huaja*, or foreign manifestations" (Tochka 2016, 2). As Nicholas Tochka has argued, this was not done out of blind cultural chauvinism but because the state's planned economies depended on "ensuring that the aesthetic resources state-subsidized artists worked and re-worked in their musical pieces, novels, poetry, and films conformed to domestic models deemed appropriate for the moral and aesthetic cultivation of ordinary Albanians' tastes" (2016, 2).

The network of authors and translators attached to Pika pa sipërfaqe are now working to remedy this constrained legacy. Already their work has begun to create new opportunities for ordinary Albanians to encounter what Kundera (2006, 35–36), echoing Goethe, called the "larger context" of world literature. Ultimately, this was how I came to see Arlind and Ataol's vision: that the books of fiction and philosophy they published might inspire in the next generation of Albanian readers the ideas, aspirations, and forms of imagination necessary to transform a culture and society in which, as Ataol glossed the extraordinary rates of Albanian migration since 1990, "those who are intelligent enough, brave enough, or quick enough, have left."

Projects and Partnerships

At the root of Arlind and Ataol's partnership was a love of reading and a drive, as Ataol put it, "to bring new books to the Albanian reader." To understand this statement within the context of the history of reading in Albania, it is worth recalling that when the Communist Party came to power after World War II, Albania was "overwhelmingly illiterate" (Mëhilli 2017, 6). With Stalinism came mass literacy, but because the state curriculum was the only curriculum, the choices available to Albanian readers were severely constrained. The literature available during this period consisted of titles approved for translation (though often with certain parts, passages, and even individual words removed) and of the works of Albanian Socialist Realism penned by the state-appointed and heavily scrutinized Albanian authors of the twentieth century.[21]

That situation began to change with the fall of communism. But the definitive transformation of Albania's literary landscape took place not in the turbulent 1990s but during the country's second decade of post-communism. Some fifteen years after the opening of markets and borders in Albania it was the entrance of online booksellers that proved decisive. As Ataol stressed in his narration, it was through internet access and Amazon that he could finally order with "one click" a book that otherwise would have been difficult to obtain by any means.

Both before and after the clicking, buying, shipping, and waiting, of course, the social dimensions of Ataol's reading were very significant. He and Arlind talked about what they were reading. They passed books back and forth. From these everyday practices of reading and discussion they formed a friendship, a business partnership, and a publishing venture that has not only transformed their experiential world but has also touched the lives of thousands of readers beyond their immediate network.

Here I think again of my conversations with Diana Malaj of the community organization ATA. In 2017, when we first met, I asked Diana about the provenance of the small library she helped to establish for ATA's headquarters in Kamëz. "The collection consists of one hundred books we received through donations," she said, "and one hundred books we bought from Pika pa sipërfaqe."[22] Within the overlapping physical, verbal, and literary worlds in which both the community organization and the publishing collective operated, the choice to stock ATA's library with books from Pika pa sipërfaqe made perfect sense. Grounding this "common sense" was a set of roughly shared attitudes, values, and beliefs that the members of each initiative expressed through their own distinctive commitments to social critique and social transformation.

Evidence for this was again on public display in July 2018, a year after my first meeting with Diana, when ATA hosted a symposium that featured a panel of local activists brought together to discuss Slavoj Žižek's 2016 book *Against the Double Blackmail* (trans. Arlind Manxhuka). This was the first of the prolific philosopher's books to be translated into Albanian. The book was published just a few months earlier, in May 2018, by Pika pa sipërfaqe.

One of the last times I saw Diana, in 2019, I had gone to attend a screening and discussion of *Citizen Europe*, which was announced on ATA's Facebook page. As it happened, I got the days mixed up. When I arrived, on a Friday, I found out the screening had taken place on Thursday. My mistake turned into another good opportunity for fieldwork: it gave me a chance to talk with Diana more informally. I went to check out the library and, doing some quick bookshelf math, estimated that it had doubled since 2017. The books—some 400 in all—now had spine labels. Along with the labels, there was also now a formal method for checking books out to activists and community members.

"We want to share [the books] with our activists," Diana said. "All these books are for our community."[23] I said it looked like the library had grown. "All these books are gifts," Diana said. "When we invite authors or translators, they bring copies of their books as gifts to the library." She gave the example of Krenar Zejno of Zenit Editions. "Krenar has been very generous," she said. "Pika pa sipërfaqe and Zenit are the only two publishers now donating to the library."

Referring to the event I attended on Monday of that week, to hear the talk of Afërdita Onuzin, a local anthropologist, Diana said: "For Afërdita, it was a reading together. We had her book and two articles. That reading was the basis of the discussion." Referring to another event featuring Blerta Hyska, who translated Simone Weil (and Louis Althusser) for Pika pa sipërfaqe, Diana said: "We are grateful to her for giving us the opportunity to get to know Simone Weil. We had one activist, Marjana, who was inspired to write something in her book like that. This is the role of translation."

It occurred to me that I should donate some books to the library. I said I would like to donate a copy of Johannes Fabian's *Time and the Other*, which I had with me (not that day, but in Tirana). "Although it's in English," I said, "I think it's fitting—because you are ATA." (The Albanian pronoun *ata* means *they*, the other.) Diana agreed.

Muhabet *and Other Mediators of Ethnographic Desire*

Back in the bookstore, late in July 2015, Arlind taught me the etymology of the Albanian word *muhabet* (conversation). "It can have bad connotations," he said. "But it's a good word. Better than *flasim* (talk), and others." He then took down from the shelf a massive Albanian-English dictionary, as if this were the most natural thing to do, and pointed to the root, *habet*.

"*Habet* is from Arabic," he said. "It means love."

"Do you speak Arabic?" I asked.

"No," he said. "I tried to learn. Maybe ten years ago. But to learn a language, you need free time. Maybe in three or four years I can try again because I love Arabic."

When I followed this with a question about his broader interests in the Islamic world, he refrained from addressing his personal beliefs or religious practices but spoke lovingly of the literary world of Islam—the world of Muslim intellectuals and poets. Given that the Communist authorities in Albania banned Islamic literature, along with religion more generally, Arlind's appreciation of literary Islam seemed to me consistent with his broader embrace of authors and ideas forbidden during the communist era.

As our conversation continued, Arlind spoke of the intertwined history of Albania and Europe: "There was a chance," he said, "for Albania to bring something different to the experience of Europe. But that chance is gone. Today we are broken."

From history the conversation returned to the Albanian language and its many influences. This again came through as a story of something lost. Here Arlind spoke of the "cleansing" of Arabic, Persian, and Turkish influences on the language (including the word *muhabet* itself) during the Albanian Cultural Revolution (1966–1969).

When we finally came to the topic of reading, it was Arlind, again, who led the way. He asked what I thought about *The Curtain*, a book of essays by Milan Kundera that he had lent me the day before. I told him I started it but didn't have time to get very far. "The first thing that struck me," I said, "was the way Kundera tied the invention of the novel to an examination of humanity. It resonated with my understanding of the invention of ethnography."[24]

"Yes," Arlind said. "And not just ethnography but the modern world, modernity." Here Arlind began talking about the thesis, the central argument of the book, concerning the novel as a genre and a cultural form bound up with European conceptions of what it means to be modern.

"Another thing that struck me," I said, wanting to steer the conversation to reading practices, "was how the book could be used as a map to find more interesting authors to read."

"Yes, it's great for that," he said. "And not just as a guide to the books but how to read them. In that," Arlind continued after a pause, "Kundera is braver than academic critics."

I agreed. "He's more direct."

Returning to the idea of using a book as a map of references to other books, I then brought up one of the first titles Kundera discusses, *Don Quixote*. Arlind visibly brightened at the reference. "*Don Quixote* contains all the themes of the modern novel," he said. He spoke of plot points as if they were common knowledge, fluidly connecting Cervantes to Dostoyevsky, describing how a minor episode in the former would become the blueprint for one of the latter's great novels (*The Idiot*).[25]

Here he got up, went to the bookshelf behind me and returned with a well-read copy (in the original French) of René Girard's *Deceit, Desire, and the Novel*, from which he proceeded to recite the author's "brilliant thesis." The first part of the theory was that there must always be a mediator between a person's desire and the object of their desire. But then, eventually, the person loses sight of this and winds up desiring the mediating object instead.

There was a lesson here, I thought, for ethnography.

Meanwhile Arlind gave two examples to illustrate. The first he drew from Cervantes. The second from Proust. The first example related to don Quixote's squire, Sancho Panza, who initially desired social mobility for his daughter. At first, don Quixote was merely the mediator of that desire. It was through don Quixote that Sancho would match his daughter to nobility. But in the meantime, Sancho lost sight of the object of his original desire and began to desire what don Quixote desired.

This, I thought, was not unlike the way my project had been re-shaped—from my initial interest in ordinary reading to my eventual concern with violence, corruption, and broken institutions in Tirana.

The example from Proust concerned the gulf between imagination and experience. Before the unnamed narrator of *In Search of Lost Time* had any direct experience at the theater, he tells us, he fell in love with the classic plays through "the simple reproduction in black and white which was given them upon the printed page" (Proust 2003, 14). Alas, when he finally had the opportunity "to see Berma" in Phèdre, he was bitterly disappointed. And yet, when M. de Norpois later spoke of Mme. Berma's "perfect taste," again, through the mediator—first reading, now conversation—the narrator's abstract love returned: "It's true!" he tells himself, "what a beautiful voice, what intelligence to have chosen Phèdre! No, I have not been disappointed!" (Proust 2003, 38–39).

Again, I thought, there was a lesson here about the fetishism of that magic word, "ethnographic." But these were not thoughts I articulated at the time. It was Arlind who carried the conversation, drawing on the books that surrounded us, flipping through their pages, locating treasured passages, his finger following the text as he translated the ideas of Girard, Kundera, Cervantes, Proust. And through this initiation into the kinds of reading and discussion that he and Ataol together took for granted, I not only learned the deeper meaning of *muhabet*, I also began to think in new ways about the triangulated desires of anthropology's subjects, objects, and mediators.

Instead of Conclusions: Some Quixotic Reflections

In "Why We Read 'Don Quixote'" Jonathan Gharraie (2011) asks, "What does it mean to be 'quixotic' today?" The question seems apt as I reflect on this material, which so centrally concerns the passions, ethics, and ideals of readers (fig. 4.1). There was certainly something quixotic in the way Ataol described his professional trajectory: "I walked into this place looking for some old poetry journals. I ended up becoming the owner. We keep opening ourselves up to unexpected circumstances. Maybe something good will come from it. Or maybe it won't."[26]

The condensed version of all that came from this openness to the

FIGURE 4.1. Tirana quixotic—electric box street art.

unexpected was that instead of finding copies of the out-of-print journal he sought, Ataol found the live literary community within which he
formed his friendship with Arlind. Together the two poured their time
and money into the bookshop (which they brought back from the edge
of closure) and the publishing house (which they formed from little more
than a desire to keep reading interesting books). But while Pika pa sipërfaqe's reputation has continued to grow year by year, the bookstore has,
for lack of a better term, changed management.

Through a sequence of events so harrowing Cervantes himself could
have penned it, Arlind and Ataol woke up to the morning of a day in late
summer 2015 to find the doors of the bookstore locked, the locks changed,
and just like that, the shop was no longer theirs. "But that is another story
and shall be told another time."[27]

The main aims I pursued in this chapter reflect two different kinds of
reading nearby. The first refers to the intimate social practice of people
reading in conversation with one another. According to that meaning,
I wanted to show how reading together mediated Arlind's and Ataol's
social experiences, making things happen in their lives that would not

have happened through solitary reading. The second sense has a more narrowly ethnographic application; it refers to approaching the activity of reading not as an object of analysis in its own right but as a point of entry for a broader social inquiry. According to that understanding of the term, I wanted to bring out some of the ways paying attention to my interlocutors' reading practices helped me to better understand how they experienced the stresses and strains of everyday life in contemporary Albania.

In addition to these two main senses of reading nearby, however, there is still a third, which in fact comes closest to Minh-ha's original notion of speaking nearby. In an interview with Nancy Chen, Minh-ha said that speaking nearby is a speaking "that reflects on itself" (Chen 1992, 87). So in addition to considering my interlocutors' passion for reading, their ethics, their idealism, and their dream that some of the people reading the books they were publishing, the future generation, will build better institutions, I also need to reflect here on my own quixotic pursuits in biblio-ethnography.

After working earlier on street libraries in India, I went into this project on publishing in Albania. This is also a little like don Quixote, who went on one long adventure, got beat up a lot along the way, came home, and then went on another adventure, where he got beat up even more. But despite all the challenges it entails, I maintain that reading nearby can open a path to what Bronislaw Malinowski identified, one hundred years ago, as the ethnographer's "final goal" (Malinowski 1922, 25). That is, to learn from people about their social world and how they see it.

Starting from questions as simple as "What are you reading now?" I have learned about the things that mattered most to Arlind and Ataol. This included both the general (for example, the broad social reality Arlind paraphrased as *katastrofë*) and the particular (for example, the singular sting, which Ataol described in a conversation that fell outside the margins of this account, of private hospitals that demand a bribe for routine medical treatments).

Viewed in terms of René Girard's (1966, 1–52) triangular model of desire—according to which there is never a simple straight line joining the subject and object—I see now that Arlind and Ataol became the mediators of my initial desire to make reading an object of ethnography. And like the squire, Sancho Panza, who began to desire what don Quixote desired, my project was re-shaped through fieldwork. But unlike Alonso Quixano, the Good, who renounced on his deathbed the name of don Quixote saying,

"I'm sane now, free and clear-minded, without the dark shadows of ignorance the detestable books of chivalry shrouded over me" (Saavedra 2011, 1029)—I am not at all ready to foreswear reading nearby.

5

Between Conflicting Systems

E ka jeta (So it goes).

— KURT VONNEGUT, *Slaughterhouse-Five* (trans. Ataol Kaso)

Pika pa sipërfaqe was not the only enterprise Arlind and Ataol began together at the end of 2009. In the same month they formed the publishing house, they also invested in a financially precarious business located near the center of Tirana. Over the next five years, they brought the store out of bankruptcy and transformed it into a vibrant cultural institution. Seeing the popularity of the business expand, the property owner asked for a large rent increase in January 2015. The booksellers replied with the best offer they thought they could manage. So began a process of increasingly tense negotiations that culminated, in July 2015, with Arlind and Ataol locked out of the institution they had done so much to create.

In outline, the arc of this narrative is familiar, even trivial. In capitalist societies, leasehold improvements often lead to an increase of rent. In detail, however, it was devastating for the people involved. The displaced booksellers appreciated the contradictions of this situation. They saw their experience as simultaneously ordinary and tragic.

In what follows, I argue that this paradoxical way of seeing was a consequence of the shifting social order of capitalist Tirana. In other words, I approach the image of ordinary tragedy as a structure of feeling in Raymond Williams's sense of "an intersection" of feelings about the past and expectations for the future into which "an observed present is arranged" (Williams 1973, 78). In contrast to the method Williams used to support his analysis of structures of feeling in English literature and society, however, the witnesses I summon here are not extracted from published works of poetry or prose. They are verbatim statements I recorded through ethnographic operations in a now-capitalist city.

I refer to Tirana as now-capitalist—despite the compelling reasons Douglas Rogers (2010, 13–15) has given for retaining "postsocialisms" as an analytic device—to bring into sharper relief the structure of feeling I am tracing in this chapter. Working in the tradition of ethnographies that pursue local perspectives on the complex and contradictory forms of value and valuation found in socialist and postsocialist contexts, I reach back in this writing to Lila Abu-Lughod's call to "experiment with narrative ethnographies of the particular" (Abu-Lughod 1991, 153).[1]

By foregrounding Ataol's interpretation of his own experience, I intend to subvert—not to reinforce—the image of a coherent "culture" of Albanian society. In this, my approach here aligns with the perspective and sentiments that Ataol himself expressed when he said, "I don't feel comfortable talking about other people's lives and actions. To some degree it would involve a unilateral act on my part, which is very close to a violent act. It would require me to speak of other people from a certain point, which is my viewpoint. And I mistrust that of course."[2]

To situate the ethnographic material included here in a meaningful context, however, I not only need to talk about other people's lives and actions; I need to refer to people and places that anyone who is familiar with the "particular social setting" I describe may well recognize. To balance my ethical obligations to the subjects and the audience of this ethnography, I will continue to use the real names of the main participants but will now use common nouns such as "the bookstore" and "the property owner" for the other Tirana people and places I discuss. This is not to preserve anonymity, which is impossible in this case. Rather, it is to distinguish between the subjects with whom I had a direct personal relationship and those I am representing here through second-hand accounts that I do not claim to have substantiated.

Believing that the effects of large-scale processes, including transformations of post-communist states, "are only manifested locally and specifically, produced in the actions of individuals living their particular lives, inscribed in their bodies and their words" (Abu-Lughod 1991, 150), the analysis I offer here conforms closely to the interpretation Ataol offered as he concluded the narration I recorded in his office in 2016.

"I don't know what you'll make of it," he said, "but I think there's a thread going through the bookstore and what happened with the publishing house and what our intentions were in the beginning and how it all collapsed." Taking that thread to be spun from the conflicting social, moral, and economic codes and conventions governing everyday life in Tirana, I see the tragedy of the booksellers' sudden eviction as an ordinary consequence of the complex interaction and conflict of values in Albania's long transformation to a capitalist order.

An Ordinary Tragedy

In July 2015, Ataol got a message from the owner of the property he and Arlind had leased since 2009. The message said, "We need to discuss something very important about the bookstore." The important thing was that the booksellers had to be out by the end of the week. A year later, in the nondescript office where the displaced tenants had relocated, I recorded Ataol's narration of the events surrounding what happened at the bookstore and why, in his words, it "failed so tragically." Losing the bookstore, Ataol said, was just part of what it meant to live "in a place like this." Sensing, correctly, that I was not yet in "a position to comprehend" (Rosaldo 1989, 7), he went on to explain,

> You know Albania some. If you knew it some more, you would probably understand better. But I think you can fairly well understand what I mean. We live in a place without rules. There are no rules here. It's a version of the jungle. A soft version. It's not complete lawlessness. But in the end, how this place works is like this: The strongest prevail. If you have enough money and enough power and if you can exert violence, you have justice with you. You can do whatever you want. Harm whomever you want. We live in a place without rules.

While this Hobbesian vision seemed very different from the warm social world I had come to know during my time in Tirana, the atmosphere of mistrust Ataol described has been well substantiated in Albanian studies. Indeed, the vernacular expression *jeta është luftë*, life is war—which some readers may know from the title of Shannon Woodcock's oral history *Life Is War: Surviving Dictatorship in Communist Albania* (2016)—goes a long way toward contextualizing Ataol's vision of living amid violence and chaos.³ Smoki Musaraj's (2018) account of corruption and "the banal intimacies of anti-corruption" likewise shows that Ataol's views about the rule of law in contemporary Albania were widely shared and corroborated nightly in the local popular media.⁴

What interests me in this social vision, however, is not its existence as such but the tension that emerges between Ataol's resignation to the inevitabilities of living in a place without rules and his simultaneous experience of these conditions as tragic and disturbing. To him this tragedy was ordinary. But how can that be? How does tragedy become ordinary? How did he and the other members of his community come to accept the persistent threat of loss and eviction? How did they come to believe that "it's not the one who's right but the one who pays the judges," that "our loss was unrecoverable," that "we can't do this," "we can't fight this," "it's pointless," "we've lost"?

All these phrases speak to a way of seeing Tirana, to a structure of feeling permeating a city and a country situated between the real social history of a harsh Stalinist dictatorship and an uncertain capitalist future. This chapter represents my effort to make sense of the constant paradox of this social vision, which of course in reality is in constant flux, and to explicate some of the broader meanings in its apparent contradictions.

Reading Nearby, Again

The core question driving this analysis can be put like this: How can something be both routine and tragic at the same time? This question recalls for me one of the more uncomfortable ironies of classic (salvage) and contemporary (urgent) ethnography. That is, as I remarked in milder terms in the last chapter, that what is conceptually or methodologically "good for the ethnographer" is often disastrous for the subjects of the account.⁵ In the present case, what was viscerally tragic for Arlind and Ataol was for me an invitation for ethnography. Ataol's response to a developed draft of the written account made this clear: "It's still uneasy for me to even think about this story, and reading about it, although in a 'cold' and 'analytic' language, makes the blood rush to my head."⁶

In practical terms, the loss of the bookstore also meant the closing of an ideal field site. For though a version of the "little book corner" was still open for business when I returned to Tirana in 2016, my days of drinking pots of tea while engaging in *muhabet* there were now over. And so, after trying without success to "drop in" at the registered address listed on the Facebook page the two friends had created for their publishing company, I texted Arlind to say I was back in Tirana, to see if he was available to meet, and to ask for directions to their new office. Arlind replied to say he was back in Elbasan for the day, but that Ataol would be there, and I was welcome to stop by. As it turned out, their new office was a place I knew from the year before, when I helped with that emergency transfer of books. The unexpected discovery of water damage in a storeroom at the bookstore, which had induced the cross-town move, was evidently a harbinger of worse things to come.

"Do you remember how to get there?" Arlind said.

I said I did. But despite being familiar with the main roads in the area, I lost myself for a good twenty minutes walking in a labyrinth of small lanes before I finally came to the place. Situated in a row of shops that included a notary public, a cleaning supply wholesaler, a medical supply distributor, and a generic café frequented by what seemed to be no more than three or four regular customers, it was the kind of nondescript storefront, common in many cities, that would be secured nightly by downing the shutters. There was no sign and no number, just three frosted glass panels (the middle one being the door) set in the drab concrete façade of an old apartment block.

Feeling less than certain that this was indeed the place, I knocked on the door. Ataol greeted me a moment later and showed me inside. He and Arlind had continued to use half of the space as a kind of warehouse for books. The hundreds we had transported the year before appeared to have grown to the thousands, many still wrapped in paper from the printer, stacked from floor to ceiling on industrial-grade shelving. By now they had converted the other side of the space to a minimalist office, with two desks positioned lengthwise along the wall, two chairs, two PCs, and more crammed bookshelves overhead.

Past this was a small lounge area with a comfortable couch, where I sat down surrounded by stacks of an ever-rotating collection of books. Instead of engaging in free-flowing conversation and writing fieldnotes afterward as I had done on previous occasions, I brought out the outline of the topics

I wanted to go over and asked for permission to record an interview. It took me about four minutes to run through the questions I had prepared about publishing, audience, readership, and translation, whereupon Ataol said, "Sure, I think there's plenty to say about all the points."

For the next fifty-five minutes I listened with interest as Ataol walked me through the past, present, and future of the publishing venture he launched in 2009 with Arlind. At the fifty-nine-minute mark in the recording I interrupted for the first time to ask, "Are there any other models? Other small publishers in Tirana that have been successful or have been established?"

This elicited a detailed (twelve-minute) response and brought our discourse to a dead end. In the slightly awkward silence that followed, Ataol said, "Later, at the end of your questions, if you want, it will be very interesting for you to understand the dynamic of how what we did with the publishing house affected the failure of the bookstore."

"Yes," I said. "That seems very important. Let's go into that."

Nearly four hours later, as he came to the end of his eviction narrative, Ataol said, "I have spared you some spicy details. But be sure there are many other aspects to it that might tickle other people into thinking about their lives, about the meaning of their actions, about everything."

Recalling Vincent Crapanzano's (1980, 7) characterization of "Tuhami's tale" (which, according to Crapanzano, implicitly carried "Moroccan values, interpretational vectors, [and] patterns of association"), Ataol's recitation was, in his own words, "very telling of the whole reality in which we live." So while our discussion never really returned to the questions I prepared about readership and its relation to issues of translation in the Albanian market for books, in keeping with the principles of reading nearby as an ethnographic method, I learned more that day listening to what Ataol wanted to tell me—about the shared moral codes of honor, respect, and concern for community that remained intact through the tragedy—than I could have gleaned from asking one hundred more prepared questions about audience, readership, and translation.

Moral Economies

Ataol opened his story by grounding it in "the moral economy" of a Muslim café in a mostly secular city.[7] When the bookstore first opened in

2004, the original owner was a practicing Muslim. But contrary to what some locals thought—and what I believed for some time—it was not that the place had any kind of religious agenda. It was just that the first owner's religion was part of the bookstore's identity from the start.

The key thing that came out of this identity, which set the bookstore apart from comparable establishments, was the owner's decision not to sell alcohol. To clarify the significance of this point for me, Ataol drew a comparison to two similar institutions in Prishtina, the capital of Kosovo, where we had recently met during that year's annual Prishtina Book Fair. What their bookstore was to Tirana, Ataol said, Dit' e Nat' (Day and Night) and Soma were to Prishtina. But the Prishtina cafés worked on a different business model. They cultivated a club scene at night that allowed them to finance the less-profitable daytime activity of selling books and keeping the doors open to local artists and writers who used the space as an informal base of operations.

Since the original owner of the Tirana bookstore was part of a community of practicing Muslims, however, it was not acceptable for him to sell alcohol, let alone operate a nightclub.[8] This small difference in the initial conditions had major implications for the general outcome of the project. When Arlind and Ataol invested in bringing the bookstore out of bankruptcy in 2009, their main innovation, which proved successful, was to organize better and broader events—such as film screenings, literary meetings, poetry readings, and book fairs—that would bring in more people. Otherwise, they conserved the general structure of the place. Thus, in addition to keeping the name, they continued the rule of not serving alcohol. This was not a decision they took lightly. They knew that serving drinks made more business sense, but their choice reflected a broader ethical attitude:

> By not serving alcohol, we eliminated certain customers outright. Some people would just not go. "They're not selling alcohol? What are we doing there?" This created a more comfortable environment for a lot of people who were not Muslims or who didn't have any interest in religion. It was like being in a library. You could just be comfortable, get some good advice on books, get to watch some good movies, and hear about some good poets.

This description fit well with my observations. A typical exchange when someone came in went like this: Arlind asked what the customer was interested in. The customer said, "This." Arlind said, "Maybe you should read that." They talked some more. Arlind read out a poem. They both laughed. The customer left with a book of poems by Zbigniew Herbert, a Polish writer unknown to her before that day.

An important consequence of their ethical attitude was that it created the conditions for the bookstore to be valued by all sorts of people (including people like myself) who were not interested in religion but who were looking for a place to find and read and discuss good books. Although there are some aspects of this that may be familiar to anyone who has spent time in a good bookshop anywhere in the world, it is important here to consider the specifics of the bookstore in question *as a business* in the postsocialist context of Tirana.

Arlind and Ataol's shared concepts of books as valuable were specifically located in a postsocialist space built on the ruins of a particularly repressive communist past. The promise of a place where you could "be comfortable, get some good advice on books, get to watch some good movies and hear about some good poets" here represented an idealized world of new possibilities outside of capitalism or communism. But because this space, as a store, had to be capitalist, there was a crisis of meaning and value between ideologies.

As to their own ideals and principles, Ataol was very clear about what he and Arlind were trying to do: "We wanted to establish an institution—institution not only in the sense of a place but as something coming from human relations established in an ordered way. An institution that after I was no longer there would still operate according to the principles of that institution." This is what mattered most to Arlind and Ataol, and their actions throughout the tragedy were guided by the belief that creating a social institution in harmony with their values justified financial sacrifices: "If we think we are doing something important and we can also financially support ourselves while doing it," Ataol said, "we should absolutely do it, and we should be careful to conserve it. This is a treasure we have here. And we have to use it as a treasure: very carefully and intelligently. This means we have to be satisfied with little."

As it happened, the active pursuit of building a durable institution that would operate according to this kind of principle led directly to their loss of the bookstore. "The failure with that goal," Ataol said, "has something to do with the failure of me and my community to build institutions. We tried to establish something for the good of the community we live in, for the good of the people who live here, and in the end it all collapsed."

Different Opinions about an Essential Fact

There were several converging problems leading to the ordinary tragedy at the center of this narrative. The most obvious concerned the financial requirements of the family who owned the property in question. The root of the conflict between the booksellers and the property owner was that the two sides had different opinions about whether the bookstore was or was not profitable. The dispute over this essential fact brings into focus larger questions about how profit and money are given value and valued differently in postsocialist Albania. The main source of the dissonance was that while the booksellers claimed they were barely breaking even, the work they were doing gave off every appearance of success. The film screenings, literary meetings, poetry readings, and book fairs all generated enthusiastic response, in some cases drawing media attention. This generated a buzz around the store and led to noticeably increased foot traffic. More people coming in usually does mean more sales. But this doesn't automatically equal more profit.

"Although we had a lot more people coming in," Ataol explained, "we also had additional costs. We had to take on more personnel. Some other costs went up. So although we had four or five times more people coming in, we didn't have four or five times more revenue."

The owners could see the people. They could hear the buzz. Considered from their perspective, it made sense to imagine that the booksellers must be making a lot of money. And if that were true, they would be justifiably upset with their tenants for not wanting to share some of that with them. So while it would be easy to cast the owners as a kind of villain in this story, it would also be incorrect.

While my access to both the "factual surface" and "horizontal reality" (Fassin 2014, 41; Nussbaum 1990, 48) of the case was limited to my own situated ethnographic operations in the field, I feel sure that the actions of the family who owned the property were not motivated by greed or other implicit ideologies of capitalism that many in the West, myself included, may take for granted. The property owners were a large family, but not a rich one. They emerged from the era of state socialism financially precarious, and like many of their neighbors, they needed the rent from their reprivatized property just to get by.[9]

At the same time, the tensions and contradictions around the moral economy outlined earlier were borne of the property owners' choices and continued according to their expectations. "It's not that it was a request on their part for us not to sell alcohol," Ataol said. "But it was implied. It was implied that when we took up [the bookstore], we would go on doing pretty much what they were doing in the first place." Given that comparable businesses in the area, which was among the most expensive real estate markets in Tirana, all sold alcohol and operated nightclubs, this expectation came with an implicit understanding that it would be very unlikely for the bookstore to generate income commensurate with the market value of the property.

Keeping in Contact with These Ideas and These Books

Though it created real financial pressures for all concerned, Ataol did not present the disagreement over what constituted a fair rent as the key factor in the eviction. The main problem he emphasized in his narration had to do with the competing demands of another project—the publishing venture. Some of the tensions between ethical principles and economic realities that factored in the operation of the bookstore also surfaced in their work as publishers, as Ataol explained:

> Whereas there are some other publishers who have chosen this as a way of life and survival—as a job—my idea of what we do [in publishing] is like this: We have a concern for the truth. And we want people to figure out through contact with ideas or other people's books, to understand, to see, what the truth is. I'm aware that this truth is very problematic. No one agrees on what that is or how one should find out. But anyway, I think our work contributes to people working toward that goal, whatever that might be. And the main reason we choose to do one book and not another is because we think that people who read it will profit from it in this sense: of having a clearer idea of what their life means and why they're doing what they're doing.

Like the bookstore, then, the publishing company operated according to ideals that have little to do with conventional economic theories of value. Ataol's expression of an intense feeling for books and the thoughts within them as valuable—as something people could profit from—was located in a social world that he and the other members of his community viewed as fundamentally broken and dysfunctional. True to Williams's conception of structures of feeling, this vision came out of an intersection of historical memory and collective expectations. The past in question was one in which a single dictate of Enver Hoxha from the Fifth Party Congress (November 1966) "made it obligatory for literature and the arts to become a powerful weapon in the hands of the Party" (Pipa 1991, 33). For a better future, Arlind and Ataol likewise looked to literature for new ways of thinking.

Combining their respect for books and their desire to bring about durable change for their community, their city, and their country, Arlind and Ataol formed the publishing company with an explicitly social purpose. They wanted to introduce Albanian readers to works that were not available during communism. This was because they saw in the literature they were then reading in other languages the promise, or at least the possibility, of a better future for Albanian society. In addition to this social ideal, however, Ataol acknowledged a second, more personal force driving their actions:

> I've thought about [why all this happened] over and over. And I think the main reason is because me and Arlind wanted to keep reading. To keep reading interesting authors. And the most natural step that came after that was, you know, "I've read this great author, so I might as well show it to other people." That was a natural, logical step. But the main concern for me, I have to be sincere, was keeping- in contact- with these ideas- and these books. [Ataol punctuated this statement, his fist striking his palm, in time with the hyphenated rhythm.]

If the main issue were only the property owner's insistence on a higher rent, Arlind and Ataol may well have survived with the bookstore intact. The more intractable problem was that they couldn't satisfy the demands of managing the bookstore without neglecting their passion for reading. As Ataol explained,

> Losing contact with these books seemed like an immanent possibility. If we would have started devolving more of our time to the management of [the bookstore] and getting [more] involved in the day-to-day activity . . . it is sure that we would have lost most of our contact with the books. Living

here, I have seen this many times. You're very involved in reading literature or philosophy. Then you have to face this violent environment. You
have to survive. Get a job. Start a family. . . . And the first thing you'll drop
is reading books. There's no more time for that. Unless you're a university
professor, or your job has to do with reading books. Otherwise you'll drop
the books. You won't read. Or you'll read less and less as you grow older.
And I didn't want this to happen. I had my mind set on this. I said, "We'll
do whatever it takes not to abandon this." And the publishing house came
about because of this. It's not that we woke up one day and said, "Let's
start a publishing house." No. It was more of a natural consequence of
not wanting to lose, whatever it was, this thing we had for reading books.

As Ataol saw it, all that happened—the eviction, the breakdown of
friendships, the money they lost—all of that was a consequence of their
decision to focus on the activity of publishing instead of managing the
store. The activity of publishing here meant reading, translating, and editing books; corresponding with foreign agents; applying for funds to support translation; going to book fairs; working with designers, printers,
and booksellers; managing their social media presence, and much more
(fig. 5.1). To do this all well obviously required a major investment of
time. The same of course was true of running a lively bookstore in Tirana.

FIGURE 5.1. The activity of publishing—at a community book fair in Tirana.

In purely practical terms, their work in publishing was not compatible with the day-to-day management of the bookstore.

But there was more to it than the limits of the working day. This is what Ataol wanted to tell me in the first place when he said, "it will be very interesting for you to understand the dynamic of how what we did with the publishing house affected the failure of the bookstore." Ataol's vision of the bookstore as a durable social institution required a certain environment, a certain philosophy, and a certain way of doing things. Meanwhile the setup he and Arlind organized for doing this collapsed. The main reason that happened, he said, was that at a certain point, "what we were trying to do with the publishing house and with the cultural activities at the bookstore somehow became incompatible with all the other stuff that was going on at the bookstore."

I realize that leaving out a description of "all the other stuff" leaves a large ellipsis in this narrative. But the most I am comfortable saying here is that the essence of the ordinary tragedy, as I understood it, was not that he and Arlind had to relocate or that they lost money; it was the breakdown of trust that gradually but inevitably corrupted the social world they built on the foundation of literary principles and ethical ideals. As Ataol explained,

> I think with initiatives such as the ones at the bookstore, with trying to publish philosophy and literature, you're inherently promising something very high. It's not like you're explicitly promising, it's implicit. But what you do inspires people in a way that they're looking for the meaning of their lives through what you're publishing. . . . We wanted people coming in to get books and to gather the truth. But instead of finding truth, they would find all sorts of crooks.

Again, with respect to the crooks Ataol referred to, it will need to suffice to say that human relations among people connected to the bookstore had become increasingly permeated with forms of suspicion, mistrust, lies, conflict, envy, and irrationality. It was precisely this normalization of violence within a space they and their friends had once experienced as an "epiphany of culture" (Likmeta 2011) and "an island in the sea of the capital" (Pedrazzi 2015) that Arlind and Ataol found most disturbing. And though I, as a listener, felt some pangs of ethnographic guilt for prompting Ataol to dredge up these memories from his recent past, he reassured me:

It feels good to talk about it. That's sure. I'm not going to lie and say "I don't want to talk about it. It's all gone. It's in the past. We can't fix it anyway." I don't think that. There's a mysterious aspect of human nature that feels great satisfaction, even if no benefit may come from telling the story. There is a part of me that wants to tell this.

Owing perhaps to the therapeutic effects of telling, by the end of his recitation Ataol gestured toward a contrasting vision:

What you see here, the publishing house that we're working with right now, and the office we have here, are some sort of retreat. This is how I see it. Our work in this office as a retreat from the world out there. We were trying to confront the day-to-day life of people by what we were doing. But we're here now. We're going on with the publishing house. We had about twelve months of terrible times. But being here, now, being able to keep in contact with these books and with our readers—to come back to what you were asking at the beginning—that seems worth it to me.

Making Sense, Intersubjectively

The first time I asked what happened with the bookstore, Ataol's answer was brief: "In a poor and violent country," he said, "it is impossible to make an institution."[10] Between this pithy statement and the twenty-five-thousand-word elaboration I later recorded, my task has been to make something from the epistemological paradox that emerged from our intersubjective communication.[11]

I began with a classic ethnographic contradiction. The eviction, which the booksellers experienced as acutely tragic, was at the same time in no way sensational to them. But how can I represent something as tragic that the participants viewed as ordinary? This was my initial problem. Working through this apparent contradiction, I came to see a series of related oppositions: personal values against controlling forces, communist dictatorship against capitalist uncertainty, atheist past against resurfacing faith. All these binary representations provided a kind of dissonance that I believe is productive and, ethnographically at least, "good to think."

As a kind of ethnographic artifact, the image of ordinary tragedy appeared right on the surface of Ataol's narration. Losing the bookstore, he said from the start, was a sad but routine part of life in a society he experienced as violent and unjust. But beyond the immediate social vision of Tirana as a place without rules, the analysis here reveals a complex structure of feeling that is not outside of laws but between them. The booksellers wanted to create an institution in a capitalist city that would operate according to a logic contrary to assigning value through money. The decisive clash, therefore, was not between law and lawlessness but between the capitalist principle of profit and the value Arlind and Ataol ascribed to community and institutions, people and books, knowledge and truth.

According to this interpretation, the very qualities that made the bookstore a vibrant institution—the booksellers' ethical attitude, their attachment to the law of honor between business associates, and the value they placed on creating a safe and welcoming atmosphere—contributed directly to its failure. This is tragic. But it has also become ordinary. For a long time now it has been difficult for ordinary people being ethical, honorable, and welcoming to manage: "We manage because we cheat a bit. We do a lot of things we shouldn't be doing. No one could manage if they stuck to the law. If I invoiced all my customers, if I didn't fiddle the books, life would be impossible" (Rouch and Morin 1961). This was not Ataol talking. Or anyone from my fieldwork. It was a young car mechanic in Paris, in the summer of 1960, talking on camera, and telling the truth, for Edgar Morin and Jean Rouch. And though what the mechanic said was true, it was as unremarkable then—aside from him saying so on camera—as it is commonplace in the world today.

This idea, that the ordinariness of this tragedy transcended the boundaries of Albania, first struck me in 2018, in London, where I had gone to present the paper, "High Ideals and Harsh Conditions," at the Royal Anthropological Institute conference, titled that year "Art, Materiality and Representation." This was my first attempt to translate my interpretation of Ataol's interpretation for an academic audience. Outside the conference, I spent some time with friends Smoki knew from growing up in Tirana. A married couple, they now lived in London. These friends were living comfortably in a nice part of the city. At a café near the Tate Modern, I had a good conversation with the husband. He was curious to hear about the conference. I spoke first about my panel in general terms, not sure how interested he would be to hear the details. He immediately grasped the theme and asked good questions to get me talking.

I told him my contribution drew on "a story from Albania." He was respectful of my not wanting to name names. The follow up questions he asked were not meant to find out who the booksellers were, or what bookstore I was talking about. Maybe he could tell. But I didn't think so. He wanted to know if they were "grounded" or if they were "super idealistic, radical left, anarchists."

"They had high ideals," I said, "but it wasn't a specific political ideology. More of a yearning for truth. They're realistic, not dreamers. Both are married, with small children, trying to make a living."

"It's difficult," he said. "Not just in Albania, but anywhere, to hold onto those kinds of ideals, to keep that integrity, when you have to face reality, responsibilities, provide for your family."

I agreed. The critique of Albanian society that ran through Ataol's narrative was thus not only critical of Albania's repressive communist past but also its new capitalist realism. I use the term here in Mark Fisher's (2009) understanding of "the widespread sense that not only is capitalism the only viable political and economic system, but also that it is now impossible to even imagine a coherent alternative to it" (Fisher 2009, 2). The everyday expression of this structure of feeling can be heard in the frequent exhortations to "be realistic" and "use common sense." These everyday expressions, as Alison Shonkwiler and Leigh Clair La Berge have noted, are "now part of the ideological enforcement process of neoliberalism" (Shonkwiler and La Berge 2014, 1). It may well be that in places where landlord-tenant law is more firmly embedded, the displaced get more time to leave, but the result is still the same. The rent always goes up, and eventually the leaseholder gets pushed out. The problem, then, was not the apparent dysfunction of Albanian society but the actual functioning of Albanian capitalism.

It Happens All the Time

I return now to that fateful message from July 2015. Within hours of hearing that the property owner wanted to discuss "something very important about the bookstore," Ataol said he already knew the business was lost. He set a meeting with the owner to explain that he and Arlind needed at least a month (rather than just one week) to pay what they owed to the vendors and publishers, to close the wages for the workers, and to get their stuff and find somewhere to put it. The initial meeting did not end well, but the owner agreed to meet a few days later to continue negotiations. The second meeting didn't go any better than the first.

How could it? The bookstore was built on the ruins of a situation that was tragic at birth. Tragic in ways that require a vision of the bookstore as a palimpsest of history in a city that has been transformed—in just one hundred years—from a sleepy town under Ottoman rule, to the capital of a modern secular state, to a city under Fascist occupation, to the political center of a Stalinist dictatorship, to a frenetic "place without rules." It was precisely with this kind of layered, archaeological vision of his city that Arlind—who read an earlier draft of this account and offered suggestions for revision as we rode bikes through Tirana traffic—said, "The details [which I have mostly now deleted] don't matter. They only matter to us because it happened to us. They wouldn't be interesting to the wider public."[12]

"Okay," I said as we stopped behind a municipal bus at a red light, "But what about what Ataol said—that this story is telling of 'the whole reality' in which you live?"

"Yes," Arlind said, "but it isn't interesting. It happens all the time."

My argument has been that the reverse is at least as plausible. This tragedy is interesting *because* it happens all the time. Though the specific details of any ordinary tragedy will, of course, depend on the time and the place of its occurrence, as a general social phenomenon, tragedies of this kind require only that people accept the unthinkable as a matter of course. My position, therefore, is that the paradox of ordinary tragedy that mediated Arlind and Ataol's vision of their city can be found not just in Tirana, or Albania, or the former socialist cities of Europe. Rather, they can be found wherever durable systems of meaning are suddenly devalued, contested, and rendered confusing. That is to say, wherever people are trying to manage their lives between conflicting systems of values.

Quixotic Redux: The Dangers and Responsibilities of Reading

In 2017, one year after I recorded Ataol's eviction narrative, I asked Arlind and Ataol how they felt about the day-to-day aspect of their current work. Their response moved, as was customary, from concrete references to a broad critique of contemporary conditions in Albania. The short answer was "Yes." They were enjoying the day-to-day work.

"In a way," Ataol said, "our current situation is better [than the situation at the bookstore], because we can concentrate on publishing, whereas before there were always one hundred other things drawing us away."[13]

They said they were still thinking about opening another bookstore. But this was not something they could do now. "Maybe in the future it will be possible," Arlind said. Until then, they would remain in their "retreat"—tucked away, in an unmarked space.

"We refer to this place sometimes as our cave," Ataol said. "This is not the way we would like to be. We would like to be public. We would like to be open. We are doing something for the benefit of society."

Arlind and Ataol told me they felt safer in their current situation—working more or less underground—than they did when they were facing the public at the bookstore. To me, this reflected another kind of ordinary tragedy, which my interlocutors described more obliquely, with reference to a constellation of dangers they associated with literature and books "in a place like Albania." To explain, Arlind referred to himself and Ataol, with self-deprecating humor, as Sancho Panza and Don Quixote.

"Does that make you Sancho?" I asked Arlind.

"Yes," he said.

"It's funny to be called Don Quixote," Ataol said. "But it's not a good thing, really."

I agreed. "I don't think what you're doing can be seen as succumbing to the dangers of idle reading," I said. "I feel like your work speaks to the responsibility of pursuing new ideas."

"This is the practical moral function of literature," Ataol said. "But there are other dangers: Misunderstanding. Misappropriating. Endless regression."

If the first of these was "not getting it" and the second was "using it for ill," the third went something like this: Because I read this, I have to read that. Because I read that, I have to read the other. And so on, forever.

A Good Time to Read

A book with theory visible is like an object with the price tag left on it.
— PROUST, *In Search of Lost Time*, vol. VI: *Time Regained*

I started reading *The Guermantes Way*, the third volume of *In Search of Lost Time*, on a plane in transit to Tirana, in summer 2019. I brought the first volume with me to read in the summer of 2017. In 2018, it was the second volume. What inspired me, without any doubt, was talking about books with Arlind and Ataol. I liked the idea of spreading the reading out over the span of a long-term research project and figured I would complete both in Tirana in 2022.

In fall 2019, I presented a paper titled "Places of Memory, Art, and Contestation," at the American Anthropological Association's annual meeting, which took place in Vancouver, Canada. An acquisitions editor for Vanderbilt University Press saw the abstract in the conference program and wrote to me saying, "Your AAA presentation caught my eye this morning and I was wondering if we might meet up to talk about a monograph." That meeting led to a book proposal for *Tirana Modern*. It looked like I would need to complete the project before I could finish reading *In Search of Lost Time*. But along with so much else, the ongoing COVID-19 pandemic reshaped that expectation.

After an uplifting talk with Arlind via WhatsApp on June 19, 2020, I started reading the fourth volume and decided he was right, "It was a good time to read." I ended up finishing *Time Regained*, the final volume of the novel, by the end of that first pandemic summer. Despite the isolation, my enjoyment of the reading was considerable. But more than the enjoyment I derived from solitary reading, the really important thing I learned from Arlind that day was that my old method, reading nearby, was also compatible with the work of ethnography from a distance.

Tirana Calling

On the call, Arlind sounded upbeat. He was at home, cooking dinner. It was 8:30 p.m. in Tirana. He said he'd been working through the COVID interruptions. He was locked down for two or three weeks at the end of March and beginning of April. But since then, he said, he had been going to the office, working, reading, talking with Ataol, Orges, and Eligers.

"During the lockdown," he said, "the number of cases was not very high. But after opening, there has been an increase in new cases. This was expected. But there are a lot of problems in managing public health here. Otherwise, life goes on. It's not a very dangerous situation [for us]. We stay together. We don't meet a lot of people."[1]

Since the start of the pandemic, Arlind said, he had been able to complete several projects, including the pagination and layout for a new book of essays by Bolaño and three new novels by Arlt. But outside of this, he said, there has been "a lot of confusion." It was not just the pandemic. As was the case in the United States and many other parts of the world, in the time of the coronavirus there were overlapping crises. The political situation in Tirana, which had been growing increasingly tense on its own, was then being compounded by reverberations from what Arlind referred to as "the political crisis in Kosovo."

It was not the political crisis, however, but the current pandemic virus that led the annual book fair in Prishtina to be cancelled.[2] Despite the real hardship this must have caused, Arlind seemed to take as much solace from reading and books as he did in ordinary times. "We're working on the books," he said. "We have a lot of new books that we are planning to publish." He then told me about some of the many books he was reading. "It's a good time to read," he said. "When you come, the new topic is Borges. My main occupation has been with Borges. I'm reviewing a translation now. All his stories are fantastic. I read all his interviews. I just finished biographies of Borges and Bruno Shultz, another author we have published. I started one on Sigmund Freud. It's very interesting."

I asked how everyone was doing. "My family, Ataol's family, everyone is fine. Ataol is working on translating *The Book of Laughter and Forgetting*. Orges and Eligers worked during the lockdown, shipping books by post.[3] Mihal and the guys on the street were locked down. From May they started working again. Bookstores and booksellers weren't closed. We [meaning Arlind, Eligers, and Orges] didn't stop collecting. Prices on Amazon and Abe books have gone very high. The shipping price and time to ship were impediments."

At the time, Arlind explained, it took three months to get books from the international sellers. But beyond the economic problem, and despite his general assessment that "things are fine," I could tell he was dealing with a lot of stress. Though again, this was not something new. "More difficult times will likely come for the economy," he said. "Let's see. People are worried about the political climate. The state is not supportive. They destroyed the National Theatre. There was a lot of outrage about that, how they did it, in an arbitrary mode, at four in the morning, with a rude confrontation.[4] I feel very depressed about the aggressive political climate. How political power is used arbitrarily. How the media is aggravating the political crisis."

Although Arlind described detailed scenes of the worsening political climate, the conversation overall, as I said, was uplifting. Yes, he saw on the horizon that more difficult times will likely come. "But," he said, "let's hope for new things. Let's hope for good."

Talking with Arlind reminded me once more of reading Sherry Ortner's (2016) synthesis of dark anthropology and anthropology of the good. He saw very clearly and felt very deeply "the ugly realities" of the world today. "If you come here," he said, "you will find the same Tirana. Next year is an election year. All the political parties are starting their propaganda." But I repeat, he remained hopeful about the potential for change.

I told Arlind that I had been feeling pretty low before talking to him that day. "We can keep in touch," he said. "You know my work schedule. Ten to five at the office. Call any day around 5:00. It's better if I talk from the office. We have Wi-Fi there. At home, the internet is not good."[5]

Correspondence from the Second Wave

In early January 2021, I received an email from Ataol. "I imagine the last couple of days to have been quite hard," he wrote. "I have no relations to US politics, but the events of Jan 6 gave me genuine anxiety, sleeplessness, and ultimately a nice migraine that I'm still digesting as I write."[6] He asked how I'd been and if "this second season of the pandemic [had been] harder than the last?" He related that everything in Tirana was mostly open. Since the lockdown ended, he wrote, "people are just getting sick." His mom got sick back in November, he said. "She was lucky. Many of her colleagues have died in the last couple of months."

He said Arlind was doing okay, but that they were both a bit depressed as the publishing activity has slowed down due to the pandemic. "Many books we were planning to publish this year have been postponed to nobody-knows-when," he said. "And 2021 seems to be headed in the same direction as this past year—the vaccine will probably be available for all the population very late in the year, maybe as far as 2022 they're saying."

When I wrote back, eight days later, I began by apologizing for my delay. I told a little about how and what I was doing. "Over the winter break," I said, "I was able to get back to writing from my fieldnotes. Doing that always makes me feel like I'm going back into conversations with you and Arlind, which is something I like very much. On the days when the writing goes well, I feel much better overall."

Three weeks later, Ataol replied. "I apologize in turn for *my* delay in response," he wrote. "It seems as if the more things slow down, the more engaged and overfilled my mind is, and I am unable to sit and write, although I have little to do beside responding to some emails and working on a book I'm editing for publication."[7] Ataol said he was glad to hear that I had been somewhat isolated from "all the shit that was going down in the US," and most importantly, that I had been able to write. "What's your next project with the notes?" he wanted to know. "Are you writing something larger?"

When I wrote back to Ataol, I described in detail what I was working on. At the end of the long description, I said I hoped to "keep building some momentum toward something bigger." I didn't say I hoped that something bigger would be a book. There was a part of me that wanted to, but that part was silenced by the insecurities of *das Ich*, "the I." What if the book doesn't materialize? In any case, Ataol's reply continued:

The situation with the publishing house is very grim right now. We're on pause with the publications. The [cancelled] book fairs killed us last year, and 2021 is still looking like an uphill path. Although we're still working on the texts, we're not sending the books to the press, because that would require money we don't have right now. There are exceptions—cases where the publication is paid for, but there are too many other books that need an upfront sum to get going, and right now we're stuck. We have no idea how and if we're going to pick up the momentum we had before the pandemic. Although we'll eventually publish some of the books waiting in line, we might not be able to do what we were doing before. And to think that we thought we already were in a dire situation . . . The moral of life in Albania, one of the main threads, at least, seems to be: there's always worse, and it's coming right at you.

As often happened in our face-to-face conversations over the period of this fieldwork, Ataol pivoted in this correspondence from an initial focus concerning books to a diagnosis of the general social and political situation in Tirana.

Other factors have contributed to worsen our state of mind. The construction mafia is booming like never before in the history of the city. There are buildings popping up practically everywhere. I have two huge high-rises exactly next to my house. We hardly slept this summer due to the noise. At times it really felt like that frog in the experiment where they raise the temperature while it is in a pan full of water, and eventually it boils without making as much as a budge. That's it: all seems to be boiling around us, and we're the frog that can't do anything but stay put and slowly boil to death.

But again, as Arlind had done in our phone call, Ataol pivoted back, from experiences befitting dark anthropology to perspectives belonging to an anthropology of the good. Being concerned with the truth, Ataol did not frame "the good" as an escape from, but as a way to make sense of the harsher dimensions of human experience.

On a positive note, I have been able to read some in the past year. I started and finished Thucydides—a wild experience! I was reading of the epidemic in Athens during the Peloponnesian war while being in an epidemic myself. Things have obviously changed since the fourth century B.C., but not that much. I already knew from Thucydides alone that the pandemic will take more than one year to pass, in spite of vaccination and all.

I sent my next reply nine days later. "I think now," I wrote, "rather than being delayed, we can just say our correspondence is following its own rhythm."

Retrospect and Summary

The point of intrigue I pursued through fieldwork between 2015 and 2021 was to understand how two Tirana residents who were born in the last days of the former dictatorship saw their world and the role and meaning of literature within it. In writing from my fieldnotes, I developed the concepts of biblio-ethnography (a writing of the relationship between books and people) and reading nearby (taking literate activity as a point of entry rather than as the object of analysis) as contributions to the broader fields of literary and media anthropology. Starting from Lila Abu-Lughod's (1991) call for writing ethnographies of the particular, Alisse Waterston's (2019) dialectic vision of intimate ethnography, Robert Darnton's (1982) view of books as a medium of communication, Arjun Appadurai's (1986a) perspective on the social life of things, David Sneath, Martin Holbraad, and Morten Axel Pedersen's (2009) concept of technologies of imagination, and the site-specific methods of observation and intervention introduced to me through Ger Duijzings's (2018) presentation, "Engaged Urbanism: Situated & Experimental Methodologies for Fairer Cities," I set out to write a Latourian account of what people do with (and in relation to) books and what books do with (and in relation to) people.

My aim was to assemble and write down some of the extratextual stories and histories that spilled off the visible surfaces of books as they moved from one point to another, creating new potentialities in the lives of the people who came into contact with them within the spatialized time of an "urban now."[8] What I found was that my interlocutors' reading and conversations with other readers mediated their experience, motivated their action, and produced, through a network of transnational actors and institutions, a small publishing house that has begun, through its own unpredictable agency, to make a difference in the public life of a rapidly changing city. And though I can't say the publishers' vision of the future is optimistic, I can say that they have managed now for more than a decade to live according to their values, to publish good books, and to enjoy the work they do.

At this point, rather than presenting my conclusions with the kind of "Exactitude in Science" that Borges depicted with the image of "a Map of the Empire whose size was that of the Empire" (1999, 325), I have in mind something closer to the message I took from another one of Borges's fictions, "Pierre Menard, Author of the Quixote." The point of that story as I understood it was that in reconstructing Cervantes's *Quixote*, word for word, the modern *Symboliste* from Nîmes, a devotee of Poe, "who begat Baudelaire, who begat Mallarmé, who begat Valéry" (1999, 92), transformed it. But, really, it wasn't Menard who transformed it. It was time and the attention of good readers to all that changed from the early seventeenth century to the 1930s. "The Cervantes text and the Menard text are verbally identical," Borges writes, "but the second is almost infinitely richer" (1999, 94). Why? Because "the 'final' Quixote [is] a kind of palimpsest, in which the traces—faint but not undecipherable—of our friend's 'previous' text must shine through" (95).

Returning now to the first question Ataol asked me in his correspondence from February 7, 2021 ("What's your next project with the notes?"), I related that I had been writing from the interview we recorded together the day before I left Tirana in 2019, which concerned the cultural translation of *i pavarur*—independent, *jofitimprurës*—nonprofit, and *social*—social. "As I was thinking through how that [cultural translation] might go," I wrote to Ataol, "I kept returning to the idea of structures of feeling from Raymond Williams" and described how that inspired me "to try to do something Williams-esque" with the way he and Arlind described their concepts to me with reference to the history of book publishing in Albania and the future orientation of what they have been doing since 2009.

I described, further, how I had been drawing on secondary sources like Peter Prifti's 1978 book *Socialist Albania Since 1944*, Robert Elsie's multivolume histories of Albanian literature (1995 and 2005), Arshi Pipa's 1991 book *Contemporary Albanian Literature*, and a series called *Discourses of Collective Identity in Central and Southeast Europe, 1770–1945*, which I noted was available for free online, although I had copied and printed the relevant sections from books I borrowed through my university library. The series contains translations, commentaries, and contextual information on figures like Naum Veqilharxhi, Pashko Vasa, and Sami Frashëri, all of which I drew on for this account.

On the question of future orientation—about where their work was going, what it was making or assembling, and how I was trying to trace all these associations through the busy intersection of the present—I told Ataol I was using ideas from Bruno Latour. Latour, I said, "also does a kind of re-translation of the terms Actor, Network, and Social."[9] And though I felt awkward talking about Ataol at the same time that I was talking to him, I went on to say:

> I approach Pika pa sipërfaqe as an actor that has mobilized thousands of other agents, including readers, translators, printers, sellers, etc., and have been tracing a particular trail of associations that began with you and Arlind reading and talking about books like *Testaments Betrayed*. . . . One of the things I've continued to struggle with, which you vividly expressed with the image of a frog in a pan, is how to connect these more abstract kinds of associations to the real conditions of your everyday life. (Sent via Gmail, 2/16/2021 9:36 p.m.)

Reading back what I wrote to Ataol about how difficult it was for me to reconstruct from my experience what participating in everyday life in Tirana was actually like, I am reminded of another passage from *Testaments Betrayed*:

> What is a conversation in real life, in the concreteness of the present moment? We don't know. All we know is that conversations on the stage, in a novel, or even on the radio are not like a real conversation. . . . *in real life*: dialogue is surrounded by dailiness, which interrupts it, slows it down . . . *in real life*: [dialogue] remains enigmatic, a thin veneer of the said over the immensity of the unsaid . . . *in real life*: the characters return to a subject already discussed, repeat themselves, correct what they just said. (Kundera 1996, 133)

Mediators All the Way Down

In spring 2021, again on WhatsApp, Arlind reported some good news. "I hold in my hand a new title," he said, referring to *Marxism and Christianity* by Alasdair McIntyre (trans. Genc Shehu, 2021). "It just came out from printing. The second book published this year."

Of the book Arlind and Ataol picked up from their printing partner, West Print, less than an hour before our call, Arlind said: "It was hard work. I've worked on this the last three months. Comparing the translation with Spanish and Italian editions. There was a lot of difficult terminology."

I asked how the project to translate the book came about.

"Years ago I bought a book by the same author at Adrion [which the reader will recall is a large bookstore based in Tirana that carries a selection of books in foreign languages]. A friend also recommended another title from this author, which I read. Later, I decided to read this [*Marxism and Christianity*]. I liked it. It was short. And it was something which has a connection with our reality here. It was a revelation for us. So I recommended it to a translator [Genc Shehu]."[10]

I asked about the main argument of the book. "In the author's account," Arlind said, "Marxism and Christianity are related. Not just because Marx borrowed concepts from Christianity but because, in the author's view, Marxism is a secularized religion. In his account, Marxism is seen as the last project of humanism. The last attempt to explain human life in general terms. It suggests we can learn from Marxism a lot of things: How to deal with injustice, inequality. That's why. To be aware of what is going on around us. Many social groups are unaware. [A book like this] gives some instruments to understand inequality."

Arlind mentioned that he had been reading more from Robert Darnton, an author we had discussed previously. "I am now reading a short history of ethics," he said. I didn't catch the title. "It's difficult but interesting. What about you? What are you reading?"

I told Arlind about Hortense Powdermaker's Hollywood ethnography from the 1940s and how that led me to Ortner's *Not Hollywood*. I said my interest in those books came from the sense I had that the ethnography I was writing was similar. Although I started out wanting to examine Albanian literary culture from an anthropological perspective, through the process of writing the account, I came to see it more as a study in media production. I asked Arlind what he thought of that.

"We have exercised a kind of influence in our society," he said. "During the last ten, eleven years we have circulated a lot of books—and not only our titles. At the book fairs, especially in Kosovo, we chose books from other independent and underground publishing houses to circulate . . .

The public now has expectations from us. They expect good titles, good books, for example from political philosophy . . . This is our media. Creating an image. Generating interest . . . A good philosophical title can create its own public. Albania and Kosovo didn't have these titles. But now there is interest, expectation, a new market. That's my account of this media."

Listening to Arlind, I thought his words could make a proper conclusion for this book. But considering, after all, that books are technologies of imagination that "precipitate outcomes that they do not fully condition" (Sneath et al. 2009, 25), I am not sure the narrative loop of a biblio-ethnography really needs to close. What I am sure about is that I want there to be more biblio-ethnographies. I want to read other situated, empirical, and intersubjective—that is to say, ethnographic—accounts of other writings of other relationships between other books and other people. Just considering the possible afterlives of the books Pika pa sipërfaqe has already put into circulation, the material that formed the basis for writing *Tirana Modern* is very far from being exhausted.

But the book you are reading is about to finish. It was a trial. I took a risk. I wanted to do an anthropological analysis of some of the books published in Tirana by a small press that seemed to be doing important work in the public interest. With Latour, I wanted "to see whether the *event* of the social could be extended all the way to the *event* of reading through the medium of the text" (Latour 2005, 133). I asked you up front if a book had ever changed the course of your life, and if one had, I prompted you to consider how. Did the change it produce lead to something unexpected?

Turning the question now back on myself, unequivocally, the answer is yes. What if I had not first encountered Latour, with *The Pasteurization of France*, many years ago? What if I had not encountered Duijzings with his talk about *Engaged Urbanism* in 2018? And Williams, who asked the reader of *The Country and the City*, apropos of the problem of perspective to which we have now returned, "Where indeed shall we go, before the escalator stops?" (Williams 1973, 11). The whole course of this work, which is inseparable from the whole course of my life, was transformed through such encounters with books.

But to prevent this account from going into an endless regression, I want to reach back once more, and not arbitrarily, to Liisa Malkki's reflections on reading matter out of place. Referring to a copy of *The Red and the Black* that belonged to her one-time informant, the political leader Gahutu Rémi, and a well-read copy of *The Catcher in the Rye* that was spotted by a foreign correspondent covering the Persian Gulf War in 1991, Malkki wrote,

> These books have stayed on in my thoughts and now present themselves as images of what anthropology's fieldwork has so often missed. They speak to the existence of accidental communities of memory, but also communities of imagination [that tend to reach] over and through categorical identities and pure locations, beyond families and national communities. Like people one might meet through accidents of history, they offer something important, a connection of value. (1997, 100)

A mediator if ever there was one, Malkki's contribution to *Anthropological Locations* (Gupta and Ferguson 1997), though it had no obvious connection to my then-current interest in New York City as a Symbolist's forest of analogy, led me, through the further mediation of scholars like Jonathan Boyarin (1993a) and mentors like Carol Breckenridge (1995), to Mr. Agavane's newspaper library on the side of Kumthekar Road in Pune, India. Through conversations there with other recent arrivals to the city such as Hemant, Umesh, and Vikas, I constructed an account of accidental communities of ordinary readers. And though I was never completely satisfied with that account, writing it transformed me. It prepared me to introduce myself to Arlind and Ataol, to form a personal connection with them, and through that connection, to write this account.

Appendix

Pika pa sipërfaqe's Catalogue of Publications, November 2009–November 2021

No.	Title *(Including English title where available)*	Author	Translator	Genre	Pages	Price *(In Lekë)*	Date
1	Thertorja pesë *(Slaughterhouse-Five)*	Kurt Vonnegut	Ataol Kaso	Fiction	276	700 L	2009
2	Gëtja mes Perëndimit dhe misticizmit oriental	Edvin Cami	n/a	Literary Studies	108	400 L	2009
3	Duke pritur lajthitjen	Adriatik Doçi	n/a	Stories	95	400 L	2010
4	Dyert e perceptimit *(The Doors of Perception)*	Aldous Huxley	Ervin Qafmolla	Essay	70	400 L	2010
5	Mishi I engjëjve *(The Flesh of Angels)*	Alda Merini	Lisandri Kola	Poetry	155	500 L	2010
6	Mirazh	Arb Elo	n/a	Poetry	140	400 L	2010
7	Vajtimi I Kalipsosë	Manjola Brahaj	n/a	Poetry	96	400 L	2010
8	Morfologjia e përrallës *(Morphology of the Folktale)*	Vladimir Propp	Agron Tufa	Literary Studies	205	1000 L	2010
9	Kultura dhe bumi *(Culture and Explosion)*	Jurij Lotman	Agron Tufa	Literary Studies	240	1000 L	2010
10	Kuja e Mnemozinës	Agron Tufa	n/a	Social Sciences	223	800 L	2010

11	Testamentet e tradhtuara (Testaments Betrayed)	Milan Kundera	Balil Gjini	Literary Studies	295	1100 L	2011
12	Misioni I intelektualit (The Vocation of the Scholar)	Johann Gottlieb Fichte	Armand Dedej	Philosophy	90	500 L	2011
13	Monadologjia (The Monadology)	G. W. Leibniz	Astrit Cani	Philosophy	63	500 L	2012
14	Vezët e thëllëzave	Rudi Erebera	n/a	Fiction	240	600 L	2012
15	Nga diktatura në demokraci (From Dictatorship to Democracy)	Gene Sharp	Gjergj Erebara	Politics	110	500 L	2012
16	Më e mira e botëve (Brave New World)	Aldous Huxley	Rudi Erebara	Fiction	211	800 L	2012
17	Tranzivore	Gerda Dalipaj	n/a	Poetry	70	400 L	2012
18	Poezi: E arta që lidh stinët	Sokol Zekaj	n/a	Poetry	432	500 L	2013
19	Të mërguarit (Exiles)	James Joyce	Davjola Ndoja	Drama	187	700 L	2012
20	Kurs i filozofisë për gjashtë orë e pesëmbëdhjetë minuta (A Guide to Philosophy in Six Hours and Fifteen Minutes)	Witold Gombrowicz	Edlira Lloha	Philosophy	120	500 L	2012
21	Pështjellimet e Tërlesit (The Confusions of Young Törless)	Robert Musil	Jonila Godole	Fiction	195	800 L	2012
22	Arti poetik (The Art of Poetry)	Nicolas Boileau	Prokok Gjergo	Literary Studies	100	500 L	2012
23	Ligjërata (Lectures)	Jorge Luis Borges	Ferida Papleka	Literary Studies	216	700 L	2013
24	Poezi (Poems)	Yves Bonnefoy	Sokol Zekaj	Poetry	210	700 L	2013

25	Traktati politik (Political Treatise)	Baruch Spinoza	Dritan Karadaku	Philosophy	195	600 L	2013
26	Arratisje nga lindja	Enis Sulstarova	n/a	Social Sciences	333	850 L	2013
27	Frikë dhe drithërimë; Përsëritja (Fear and Trembling; Repetition)	Søren Kierkegaard	Bashkim Shehu	Philosophy	286	700 L	2014
28	Ferdydurke	Witold Gombrowicz	Edlira Lloha	Fiction	313	800 L	2014
29	Stina e Hijeve	Virion Graçi	n/a	Fiction	172	600 L	2014
30	Histori (e) skatologjike	Arben Dedja	n/a	Stories	138	600 L	2014
31	Poezi: Avulli i verës	Sokol Zekaj	n/a	Poetry	431	700 L	2014
32	Shoqëria kundër shtetit: Kërkime në antropologjinë politike (Society Against the State: Essays in Political Anthropology)	Pierre Clastres	Orgest Azizi	Social Sciences	313	800 L	2014
33	Shpikja e traditës (The Invention of Tradition)	Eric Hobsbawm, Terence Ranger (eds.)	Doan Dani, Enis Sulstarova	Historical Studies	400	800 L	2015
34	Konkuista e Amerikës: Çështja e "tjetrit" (The Conquest of America: The Question of the Other)	Tzvetan Todorov	Primo Shllaku	Historical Studies	327	800 L	2015
35	Etika (Ethics)	Baruch Spinoza	Dritan Karadaku	Philosophy	520	1000 L	2015
36	Ligjërimi nacionalist në Shqipëri dhe studime të tjera	Enis Sulstarova	n/a	Social Sciences	234	800 L	2015
37	Golemi (The Golem)	Gustav Meyrink	Ervin Lani	Fiction	252	800 L	2015

38	Pavdekësia (Immortality)	Milan Kundera	Balil Gjini	Fiction	384	800 L	2015
39	Shkrime kritike (The Critical Writing of James Joyce)	James Joyce	Davjola Ndoja	Essay	258	800 L	2015
40	Pedro Paramo; Rrafshina në flakë (Pedro Paramo; The Burning Plain)	Juan Rulfo	Bajram Karabolli	Fiction; Stories	288	800 L	2015
41	Mbi përrallën (Italian Folktales)	Italo Calvino	Rigel Rizaj	Literary Studies	162	700 L	2015
42	Mëngjes kampionësh (Breakfast of Champions)	Kurt Vonnegut	Ataol Kaso	Fiction	341	800 L	2015
43	Shkrimtari dhe fantazmat e tij (The Writer in the Catastrophe of Our Time)	Ernesto Sabato	Bashkim Shehu	Literary Studies	317	800 L	2015
44	Mbi poezinë naive dhe sentimentale (On Naïve and Sentimental Poetry)	Friedrich Schiller	Armand Dedej	Literary Studies	108	800 L	2015
45	E qeshura (Laughter)	Henri Bergson	Blerina Hankollari	Philosophy	138	600 L	2015
46	Mbi dhunën (On Violence)	Hanah Arendt	Nolian Seitaj	Essay	126	500 L	2015
47	Historia e vdekjes në Perëndim (Western Attitudes Toward Death)	Philppe Ariès	Dritan Xhelo	Historical Studies	86	500 L	2015
48	Kanoa prej letre – Antropologji e teatrit (The Paper Canoe: A Guide to Theatre Anthropology)	Eugenio Barba	Romeo Kodra	Literary Studies, Theater	286	800 L	2015
49	Moderniteti dhe Holokausti (Modernity and the Holocaust)	Zygmunt Bauman	Enis Sustarova	Social Sciences	348 fq	1000 L	2015

50	Mbi televizionin (On Television)	Pierre Bourdieu	Dilfirus Vrioni	Essay	132	800 L	2015
51	Nën shenjën e modernitetit – Antropologji e proceseve proletarizuese gjatë socializmit shtetëror	Olsi Lelaj	n/a	Social Sciences	305	800 L	2015
52	Hyrje në letërsinë fantastike (The Fantastic: A Structural Approach to a Literary Genre)	Tzvetan Todorov	Gjovalin Kola	Literary Studies	207	700 L	2015
53	Poezi (Poems)	Oskar Milosz	Zimo Krutaj	Poetry	173	700 L	2015
54	Kulla e mishit	Arben Dedja	n/a	Stories and Interviews	216	700 L	2016
55	Mitologjitë (Mythologies)	Roland Barthes	Persida Asllani	Cultural Studies	300	700 L	2016
56	Tristia; Poezi (Tristia; On Poetry)	Osip Mandelshtam	Agron Tufa	Poetry, Essay	320	700 Lekë	2016
57	Shpikja e Mesjetës: Vetja dhe Tjetri në medievistikën shqiptare	Doan Dani	n/a	Historical Studies	520	1200 L	2016
58	Gjashtë drama (Festa e ditëlindjes; Dhimbje e lehtë; Mbrëmja; Kujdestari; Dashnori; Kohë të vjetra) (Six Dramas [Birthday Party; Mild Pain; Evening; Guardian; Lover; Old Times])	Harold Pinter	Rudi Erebara	Drama	354	1200 L	2016
59	Poezi (Poems)	Georg Trakl	Arb Elo	Poetry	335	700 L	2016
60	2666	Roberto Bolaño	Bashkim Shehu	Fiction	1097	1500 L	2016

61	Poezi (Poems)	Fernando Pessoa	Lisandri Kola	Poetry	192	700 L	2016
62	Antropologji e Kanunit	Nebi Bardhoshi	n/a	Social Sciences	337	1000 L	2016
63	Islamizëm do të thotë lindje': Rrëfimi i kombit, Evropës, dhe islamit në ligjërimin publik dhe në tekstet shkollore të histories	Enis Sulstarova	n/a	Social Sciences	230	800 L	2016
64	Teoria e shoqërisë (Theory of Society [Italian edition])	Niklas Luhmann with Raffaele De Giorgi	Adriana Prizreni	Social Sciences	472	1000 L	2016
65	Mbi heronjtë dhe varret (On Heroes and Tombs)	Ernesto Sabato	Bajram Karabolli	Fiction	594	1200 L	2016
66	Oda Alabastri: poezi të zgjedhura (Alabaster Chambers: Selected Poems)	Emily Dickinson	Arben Dedja	Poetry	146	700 L	2017
67	Tregime të natyrshme dhe të mbinatyrshme (Ordinary and Extraordinary Stories)	Carlos Fuentes	Bajram Karabolli	Stories	290	1000 L	2017
68	Tema të filozofisë të së drejtës (Law and Legitimacy)	Raffaele De Giorgi	Adriana Prizreni	Social Sciences	154	800 L	2017
69	Vetja dhe tjetri: Dyzet e pasë vjet të filozofisë franceze (1933–1978) (Modern French Philosophy)	Vincent Descombes	Elvis Hoxha	Philosophy	255	800 L	2017
70	Monolog mbi poezinë dhe ese të tjera (On Poetry and Other Essays)	Jorgos Seferis	Romeo Çollaku	Literary Studies	305	800 L	2017

71	VALIS	Philip K. Dick	Ataol Kaso	Fiction	314	800 L	2017
72	Poezi, 2016	Arben Idrizi	n/a	Poetry	70	500 L	2017
73	Kushti postmodern: Raport mbi situatën e dijes (The Postmodern Condition: A Report on Knowledge)	Jean-François Lyotard	Orgest Azizi	Philosophy	182	500 L	2017
74	Edukimi i stoikut: Dorëshkrimi i vetëm i baronit të Teives (The Education of the Stoic: The Only Manuscript of the Baron of Teive)	Fernando Pessoa	Esterina Celami	Fiction, Literary Studies	90	500 L	2017
75	Hegjemonia kombëtare: Studime dhe artikuj	Enis Sulstarova	n/a	Social Sciences	457	1000 L	2017
76	Armiku i popullit pa emër	Idlier Azizaj	n/a	Fiction	91	600 L	2017
77	Moderniteti i lëngët (Liquid Modernity)	Zygmunt Bauman	Dritan Xhelo	Social Sciences	309	1000 L	2017
78	Fetë e politikës: Mes demokracive dhe totalitarizmave (Politics as Religion: Between Democracies and Totalitarianisms	Emilio Gentile	Doan Dani	Social Sciences	297	1000 L	2017
79	Toka të pabanuara	Sokol Zekaj	n/a	Poetry	191	700 L	2018
80	Histori e shkurtër e estetikës (A Brief History of Aesthetics)	Elio Franzini, Maddalena Mazzocut-Mis	Eldon Gjikaj	Philosophy	201	800 L	2018
81	Armëpushimi (The Truce)	Mario Benedetti	Erion Karabolli	Fiction	178	800 L	2018

82	Kundër shantazhit të dyfishtë (Against the Double Blackmail)	Slavoj Žižek	Arlind Manxhuka	Essay	131	600 L	2018
83	Varietete të përvojës fetare: Studim i natyrës njerëzore (Varieties of Religious Experience: A Study of Human Nature)	William James	Sokol Kosta	Religious Studies	533	1500 L	2018
84	Shqiptime të rralluara: Poezi 1987–2017	Arben Dedja	n/a	Poetry	64	500 L	2018
85	Republika e Platonit (Plato's Republic)	Alain Badiou	Elvis Hoxha	Philosophy	522	1000 L	2018
86	Demokracia dhe totalitarizmi (Ese të zgjedhura) (Democracy and Totalitarianism [Selected Essays])	Claude Lefort	Muhamedin Kullashi	Philosophy	213	800 L	2018
87	Abadoni, engjëlli i skëterrës (The Angel of Darkness)	Ernesto Sabato	Erion Karabolli	Fiction	544	1200 L	2018
88	E ardhmja e një iluzioni; Ligështimi në qytetërim (The Future of an Illusion; Civilization and Its Discontents)	Sigmund Freud	Sokol Kosta	Philosophy, Psychology	217	1000 L	2018
89	Kujtime të përtejvarrit, Vëllimi 1 (Memoires from Beyond the Grave, Volume 1)	François-René de Chateaubriand	Primo Shllaku	Memoire	646	1500 L	2018
90	Rruga e krokodilëve dhe tregimet e tjera (The Street of Crocodiles and Other Stories)	Bruno Schulz	Romeo Çollaku	Stories	431	1000 L	2018

91	Ditar (Diary)	Witold Gombrowicz	Edlira Lloha	Memoire	1082	1500 L	2019
92	Saga e familjes Marks (The Marx Family Saga)	Juan Goytisolo	Bashkim Shehu	Fiction	237	1000 L	2018
93	Rëndesa dhe hiri (Gravity and Grace)	Simone Weil	Blerta Hyska	Philosophy	217	600 L	2019
94	Hyrje në filozofi për jofilozofët (Philosophy for Non-philosophers)	Louis Althusser	Blerta Hyska	Philosophy	285	1000 L	2019
95	Miti dhe realiteti (Myth and Reality)	Mircea Eliade	Azem Qazimi	Religious Studies	197	800 L	2019
96	Jeta është luftë: Mbijetesa në diktaturën komuniste shqiptare (Life Is War: Surviving Dictatorship in Communist Albania)	Shannon Woodcock	Davjola Ndoja dhe Luljeta Ikonomi	Historical Studies	245	1000 L	2019
97	E shenjta dhe profania (The Sacred and The Profane)	Mircea Eliade	Denata Qazimi dhe Azem Qazimi	Religious Studies	172	800 L	2019
98	Aliu në makth	Ejus Mezini	n/a	Drama	97	600 L	2019
99	Estetika e muzikës (Esthetics of Music)	Carl Dahlhaus	Edmir Ballgjati	Philosophy, Music	182	800 L	2019
100	Shoqëria pa shkollë (Deschooling Society)	Ivan Illich	Arjan Gjikola	Social Sciences	172	800 L	2019
101	Mendja e robëruar: Ese mbi logokracitë popullore (The Captive Mind)	Czesław Miłosz	Bashkim Shehu	Essay, Memoir	304	800 L	2019
102	Poezi (Poems)	Jorgos Seferis	Romeo Çollaku, Alket Çani	Poetry	298	800 L	2019

103	Sinagoga e ikonathyesve (The Temple of Iconoclasts)	J. Rodolfo Wilcock	Arben Dedja	Stories	201	1000 L	2019
104	Rrëfimet (Confessions)	Jean-Jacques Rousseau	Feride Papleka	Memoir	681	1500 L	2019
105	Arratisje nga Lindja: Orientalizmi shqiptar nga Naimi te Kadareja, botimi i katërt i ripunuar	Enis Sulstarova	n/a	Social Sciences	332	1000 L	2019
106	Libri i dhunës	Arben Idrizi	n/a	Stories	251	800 L	2019
107	Në parantezë (Between Parentheses)	Roberto Bolaño	Bashkim Shehu	Essay, Interviews	392	1000 L	2109
108	Qen kashte: Përsiatje mbi njerëzit dhe kafshë të tjera (Straw Dogs: Thoughts on Humans and Other Animals)	John Gray	Sokol Kosta	Philosophy	240	800 L	2020
109	Gravura nga Buenos Airesi (skica dhe tregime) (Etchings of Buenos Aires)	Roberto Arlt	Erion Karabolli	Essay, Stories	286	1000 L	2020
110	Jetë imagjinare (Imaginary Lives)	Marcel Schwob	Primo Shllaku	Stories	191	1000 L	2021
111	Krishterimi dhe marksizmi (Marxism and Christianity)	Alasdair McIntyre	Genc Shehu	Philosophy	154	900 L	2021
112	Libri Çajt (The Book of Tea)	Okakuro Kakuzo	Ervin Qafmolla	Essay	102	500 L	2021
113	Dhuna: gjashtë përsiatje të tërthorta (Violence: Six Sideways Reflections)	Slavoj Žižek	Arbër Zaimi	Philosophy	240pp	1000 L	2021
114	Zhvillime urbane: tradita dhe risi – Rasti i Kamzës	Alfred Halilaj	n/a	Social Sciences	446	1200 L	2021

| 115 | Fati i fjalëve | Irhan Jubica | n/a | Essay | 286 | 800 L | 2021 |
| 116 | Tregimet (Collected Fictions) | Jorge Luis Borges | Bashkim Shehu | Stories | 555 | 1500 L | 2021 |

Notes

1. An unabridged republication of the first edition of *Prints and Visual Communication* has been digitally preserved and made freely available by the Universal Digital Library, a searchable collection of more than one million books, available to everyone over the Internet.
2. For examples of the idea of the book as an actor in history, see Febvre and Martin (1976), Eisenstein (1983), Ginzburg (1992), Chartier (1994), Johns (1998), Sherman (2008), and Blair (2010).
3. I was not present for the exchange but am reporting it as told by the publishers, in response to my questions about how readers have responded to their work.
4. For a discussion of the neglect of ethnographic research on book reading, see Fabian (1993). For examples of ethnographies that explore book reading among children, students, religious communities, and fans of specific authors and genres, see Cochran-Smith (1984), Sarris (1993), Boyarin (1993b), Mahmood (2005), Griswold (2000), Halvorson and Hovland (2021), Reed (2011), Radway (1991), Sadana (2012), and Wiles (2015; 2021). For anthropological reflections on books in transit and transitory spaces, see Lukacs (2013) and Malkki (1997).
5. Following up with Arlind, I asked how he came into contact with the prison psychologist. "She was a client at [the bookstore] E për-7-shme," he said. "And a poet."
6. Interview conducted in Tirana, July 23, 2021.
7. For comprehensive treatments of literary anthropology as a subject area, see De Angelis (2002) and Rapport (2012). For a closer look at what is new and emergent in the subdiscipline, see Fournier and Privat (2016) and Nic Craith and Fornier (2016).
8. The essential references when speaking of anthropology as writing and interpretation are Geertz (1973a; 1988), Marcus and Cushman (1982), Clifford and Marcus (1986), and Behar and Gordon (1995).
9. Mining the pages of English novels for perspectives that could enhance his fieldwork in England, for example, Nigel Rapport (1993, 1994) provided early and influential arguments for approaching literature as a bridge to anthropology. For other examples of using literature as ethnographic source material, see Spradley and McDonough (1973), Handler and Segal (1990), and Cohen (2013).
10. For excellent and instructive examples, see Augé (2013), Jackson (2013a), Narayan (2007; 2012), Pandian and McLean (2017), Waterston and Vesperi (2009), and Wulff (2016).
11. In addition to the works listed in note 4, the key reference for me has been the 1968 collection *Literacy in Traditional Societies*, edited and introduced by Jack Goody, with contributions from Maurice Bloch, Jack Goody, Kathleen Gough, I. M. Lewis, M. Meggitt, R. S. Schofield, S. J. Tambiah, Ian Watt, and Ivor Wilks.

12. On everyday practices and tactics such as "reading as poaching" and "walking in the city," see de Certeau (1988a; 1988b). On dispersed practices in general see Schatzki (1996); for discussion of dispersed practices related to living in media saturated worlds, see Hobart (1999), Ardévol et al. (2010), and Bird (2010).
13. I discuss this method of reading nearby in more detail in Chapter 4.
14. See, for example, De Waal (2014), Lelaj (2015), Musaraj (2018; 2020), and Schwandner-Sievers (2002; 2004a; 2004b).
15. Readers who are interested in my ethnography of reading in India can see Rosen (2015; 2018).
16. I discuss the early days of fieldwork for this project in more detail in Chapter 4. The conclusion contains a discussion of how the project was reshaped by the COVID-19 pandemic. The present account also includes corrections, clarifications, and new insights I gleaned from a return to the field for dialogic editing in summer 2021.
17. Ahmet Muhtar Zogolli changed his surname to the more Albanian sounding Zogu in 1922, declared himself king in 1928, and went into exile at the start of the Italian occupation in 1939 (Halili 2013, 177).
18. I discuss the changes in ownership in more detail in Chapter 5.
19. In keeping with disciplinary conventions regarding masking and transparency in ethnographies that deal with public-facing actors such as artists and writers (Duclos 2019; Jerolmack and Murphy 2019; Reyes 2018), I do not attempt to disguise the identity of the publishers, authors, or translators I discuss in this account. I do, however, refer to some of the other actors I discuss using pseudonyms or common nouns.
20. Interview conducted in Tirana, June 18, 2018.
21. Interview conducted in Tirana, August 9, 2019.
22. OBC Transeuropa is a think tank based in Italy that reports on socio-political and cultural developments in Southeastern Europe, Turkey, and the Caucasus.
23. Interview conducted in Tirana, July 21, 2021.
24. Readers who are interested in the full list of works published by Pika pa sipërfaqe from 2009 to 2021 can see the Appendix. As an empirical resource for biblio-ethnography, a closer look through the catalogue can reveal a variety of meaningful patterns and relations that raise questions for further research. What, for example, explains the overrepresentation of writers who were displaced by political violence during the period Eric Hobsbawm (1994) called "the short twentieth century" (1914–1991)? And what, for that matter, accounts for the underrepresentation of women and non-Western writers and of texts that provide critiques of patriarchal and racialized structures of power?
25. This ratio of domestic and foreign fare is consistent with current trends in the Albanian book publishing industry (Bedalli 2013).
26. Interview conducted in Tirana, August 9, 2019.
27. Interview conducted in Tirana, July 23, 2021.
28. A small correction—E për-7-shme in 2012 was the most accessible but not the only antiquarian bookshop in Tirana.
29. Interview conducted in Tirana, June 24, 2018.
30. Interview conducted in Tirana, June 17, 2019.
31. Interview conducted in Tirana, July 22, 2017.
32. Interview conducted via WhatsApp, May 15, 2021.

33. See the About section of the press's Facebook page: https://www.facebook.com/PikaPaSiperfaqe.
34. For examples of intimate ethnography centered on personal family narratives, in addition to Waterston (2014), see Rylko-Bauer (2014), Chawla (2014), and Pandian (2014). For intimate ethnography in the broader sense in which I am using the term, see Crapanzano (1980), Behar (1993), and Jackson (2013b).
35. From media anthropology (Ginsburg, Abu-Lughod, and Larkin 2002; Rothenbuhler and Coman 2005; Wilk and Askew 2002), I have drawn most from the contributions of media practice, media production, and culture industry studies (Bräuchler and Postill 2010; Abu-Lughod 1997; Ginsburg 1995; Horkheimer and Adorno 2002; Powdermaker 1950; Mayer, Banks, and Caldwell 2009; Ortner 2013). From literary anthropology (De Angelis 2002; Rapport 2012; Nic Craith and Fournier 2016; Wiles 2020), I have engaged mainly with approaches that apply ethnographic methods to the study of socially embedded practices of reading and writing (Boyarin 1993a; Cochran-Smith 1984; Goody 1968b; Griswold 2000; Radway 1991; Reed 2011; Sadana 2012; Wiles 2015; Wiles 2021; Wulff 2017). From urban anthropology (Sennett 1969, Hannerz 1980; Low 1999; Pardo and Prato 2016; Pardo and Prato 2018), the key text for my analysis was *Engaged Urbanism: Cities Methodologies* (Campkin and Duijzings 2016).
36. Here I am mindful of the warning Alf Hornburg (2021) issued in a broader critique of "postdualist" social theory. In the effort to distribute agency to objects, Hornburg argued, we may end up, contrary to the intentions of most postdualists, naturalizing and depoliticizing the very human economies and technologies that are responsible for making the neocolonial asymmetries of global capitalism and the current climate crisis.
37. By positionality I mean how my "choices of setting and role" (Yanow 2009, 287) built on my earlier interests and experiences—as a reader, as a junior scholar invested in the anthropology and ethnography of reading, and as someone with an intimate connection to Albania. As for access, I mean how I "established and maintained relationships" over a long period of time (Yanow 2009, 288). For a fuller treatment of why I think these issues are so important, see Yanow's (2009) discussion of "the third hermeneutic," which adds the event of reading/listening to Clifford Geertz's influential perspective of ethnographic writing as "constructions of other people's constructions" (Geertz 1973b, 9).
38. In developing this anthropology of ordinary ethics, Jackson took his cues, in turn, from Levinas (1987) and Sartre (with Lévy 1996).

CHAPTER 1

1. Albania applied for EU membership in 2009 and received candidate status in 2014. In 2020, the bloc's twenty-seven member states formally consented "to start membership talks" (Baczynska 2020).
2. As the Tirana-based writer, translator, publisher, and library director Piro Misha has shown, the "national idea" of Albania was a product of the nineteenth-century social and literary movement—Rilindja Kombëtare (National Renaissance). The movement was initially restricted to "a handful of intellectuals living abroad with limited real impact" (Misha 2002, 39). By the 1870s, the movement established political aspirations inside the country. These were realized, in 1912, when Albania achieved independence after more than four hundred years of Ottoman rule.

3. Before joining the Communist Party of Albania, Enver Hoxha taught French and served as the caretaker of the library of the Albanian National Lyceum in Korça (Dervish 2016, 188)

4. Interview conducted in Tirana, August 9, 2019.

5. Because the state by law takes five copies of each publication, however, contemporary records from the National Library can give at least a rough picture of the formal section of the market. According to INSTAT (the statistical agency of Albania), the total number of new titles (including books, articles, maps, dissertations, and audio-visual materials) acquired by the National Library during the years 2018 to 2020 was 33,091 (INSTAT 2021). From those figures, I think it would be reasonable to estimate that up to 2,000 books may have been published per year in the referenced period.

6. Interview conducted in Tirana, June 30, 2017.

7. When I say this history was common knowledge to people involved in the Albanian book trade, I do not mean that they actually had all the dates and names ready to hand but that they seemed to have absorbed and internalized the categories and classifications that structure the narrative to such an extent that whatever interesting points it might suggest to a novice already appeared to them as "self-evident" (Bourdieu 1977, 164).

8. The name 8 Nëntori refers to November 8, 1941, the date the Communist Party of Albania was founded.

9. From the translation of his first novel into French in 1970 to the Booker Prize he received for a life's work in 2005, Kadare's brand of socialist realism found great success outside of Albania. Agolli's writing is far less known to international audiences, but for a concise representation of Albanian Socialist Realism elevated to art, I can think of no better example than the poem "Labor," which Agolli wrote in memory of his father. It opens with "Crumbs of earth shine blue under his nails, / crumbs from fields and lawns. / They're blue like the lines in the globe of the world, / like the violin's chords" (Pipa 1991, 31). Here Agolli invokes a "truthful, historically concrete representation of reality" (Pipa 1991, 7) not to please the Party ideologues but to express sincere love and appreciation for the land and for his father.

CHAPTER 2

1. A note about the name of the square—among other accomplishments, Fan Noli is well known in Albania today for his 1933 translation of part one of *Don Quixote* by Miguel de Cervantes. The translation is notable both for its continued popularity with contemporary Albanian readers and for its stylistic use of *shqiperimi*, the action according to the word, *shqip*, which means "Albanian." The term *shqiperimi* is an older, heavier, and literally more Albanian-ized term for *perkthim*, or translation. It was first associated with, and perhaps coined by, Noli, whose translation of *Don Quixote* included local toponyms and other features to make the novel more relatable to Albanian readers.

2. IAKSA, along with the Institutes of Archaeology, History, and Linguistics and Literature, belongs to the Academy of Albanological Studies. For an account of the prehistory of IAKSA, see Armanda Hysa's (2013) "Albanian Ethnography at the Margins of History, 1947–1991."

3. A prolific scholar, Duijzings was probably best known to the assembled audience for his (2002) essay, "Religion and the Politics of 'Albanianism': Naim Frashëri's Bektashi Writings," which appeared in the influential collection *Albanian Identities: Myth and History*, edited by Stephanie Schwanderner-Sievers and Bernd J. Fisher.

4. The Albanian National Theatre was built by the Italians in 1938. It emerged as a site of contention in 2018, when the government announced plans to demolish and replace it with a building designed by the Copenhagen- and New York-based firm Bjarke Ingels Group (Gjevor 2019).

5. To protect their identities, I use pseudonyms for most of the booksellers I discuss in this account.

6. Ever since Lévi-Strauss (1963) first made the claim for totemic animals, a veritable laundry list of anthropological topics have been deemed "good to think." Readers who are interested in a partial list can see Rosen (2015, 1061).

7. The sketch was first printed in a 1955 issue of the French weekly journal *Les Lettres Francaises*, in celebration of the 350th anniversary of the first part of Cervantes's *Don Quixote* (PabloPicasso.org 2021).

8. "In this capital city of ours," Alfred Rakipi wrote in a 2017 editorial published in *Tirana Times*, "gambling is present in every neighborhood, public space, and most of the ground floors of buildings on main and secondary streets" (Rakipi 2017). Rakipi concluded with a wish for the future: "Let's hope that the owners of the gambling shops in the city are willing to vacate the city itself. And if not, let's hope they are compelled to do so by law." Apparently, someone in the central government was listening. On January 1, 2019, Albania banned all gambling. Seemingly overnight, more than 4,000 betting shops shut down for good.

9. Interview conducted in Tirana, July 25, 2017.

10. Following the Russian convention for measuring book size, the format was designated as 70 × 100 × 32, which refers to the size of the paper sheet for printing in centimeters and fractions of sheet (70—width, 100—height, and 32—fraction).

11. Mihal Duri is remembered as a "hero of the people." In 1941, he printed the tracts of the Communist Group of Korça that were distributed in Tirana. In 1942, he was killed in the resistance against the Italian Fascist forces (Dervish 2016, 102).

12. Livadhja is a village in southern Albania. The population in 2011 was 1,165. Readers who are interested the full text of the poem in the original Albanian can see Metani (2005).

13. Interview conducted in Tirana, July 31, 2019.

14. Interview conducted via WhatsApp, June 19, 2020.

15. From Bolaño, Pika pa sipërfaqe has so far published the 1,100-page novel *2666* (2014) and the collection of essays *Between Parentheses* (2019), both translated from the original by Bashkim Shehu.

16. Gombrowicz's collected musings were originally published, between 1953 and 1969, in *Kultura*, a Polish literary magazine based in Paris.

17. See Arendt's essay, *On Violence* (1970; trans. Nolian Seitaj, 2015); and Bauman's *Modernity and the Holocaust*, (1989; trans. Enis Sulstarova, 2015) and *Liquid Modernity* (2000; trans. Dritan Xhelo, 2017).

18. ATA (lit., THEY) formed in 2014 as a group of activists operating and working in Kamëz, a recently formed city on the periphery of Tirana. In everyday talk, Tirana people often referred to Kamëz as an "informal area" because of the way many of the houses there were built—by people who came to the capital to start new lives after the fall of communism. The group took the name of the Albanian third person plural pronoun (*ata, atyre*) as a reference to what they called "the clash between the stranger within oneself and the gaze of the other from the outside" (https://www.facebook.com/grupiata).

19. Interview conducted in Kamëz, June 28, 2019.

20. I provide further analysis of the referenced conversation in Chapter 5.

CHAPTER 3

1. Interview conducted in Tirana, August 9, 2019.

2. I use the term "long conversation" in the broad sense that Maurice Bloch adopted in his (1977) reformulation of Malinowski's vision of fieldwork.

3. In other words, I saw my interlocutors' view of literature in a way that rhymed with the position Wolfgang Iser elaborated in his 1989 essay, "Toward a Literary Anthropology," wherein the literary scholar responded to the question, "Why do we [human beings] need fiction?" by saying, "Fictions are inventions enabling humankind to extend itself" (Iser 1989, 265).

4. Interview conducted in Tirana, June 15, 2018.

5. The original plan (less sexy and more pragmatic) was actually hatched by Lulsim Basha of the opposition Democratic Party (PD) when he was Tirana's mayor. But Basha's plan was blocked by the Prime Minister, Rama of the Socialist Party (PS), continuing a pattern established by the Prime Minister before him, Sali Barisha (PD), who routinely blocked Rama's plans when Rama himself was mayor of Tirana.

6. To substantiate this claim, Pipa mentions that the first Minister of the Economy, Nako Spiru, was an economics student who had not completed his studies and that the Minister of the Treasury in the first Albanian government, Ramadan Çitaku, was a land surveyor.

7. Pika pa sipërfaqe published both Alain Badiou's *Republika e Platonit* (trans. Elvis Hoxha) and Claude Lefort's *Demokracia dhe totalitarizmi* (trans. Muhamedin Kullashi) in November 2018.

8. See the Facebook page for Pika pa sipërfaqe, https://www.facebook.com/PikaPaSiperfaqe.

9. Bruno Latour has given the relevant etymology: "[In] Latin *socius* denotes a companion, an associate. From the different languages, the historical genealogy of the word 'social' is construed first as following someone, then enrolling and allying, and, lastly, having something in common" (2005, 6).

10. Interview conducted in Tirana, August 9, 2019.

11. See, for example, Benjamin (1999), Williams (1973), Bakhtin (1981), Koselleck (1985), Basso (1996), Lambek (2003), Robinson (2013), Napolitano (2015), Hartog (2016), Stewart (2016), Hodges (2019), and Musaraj (2021).

CHAPTER 4

1. By social infrastructure Long meant that "reading must be taught" and that socialization into reading "always takes place within specific social relationships" (1993, 191). By social

framing she meant that collective and institutional processes authoritatively define "what is worth reading and how to read it" (192).

2. In Cochran-Smith's study, these layers of context included "the literacy attitudes, values, and practices of the adult community . . . the general nursery-school atmosphere and environment . . . the network of literacy events that surround and support storyreading . . . [and] the immediate physical and verbal environment in which storyreading occurs" (1984, 37).

3. While my first meeting with Arlind and Ataol took place on June 15, I first referred to the bookshop in my fieldnotes a week earlier. Here is what I wrote: "8 June 2015. Project begins. Talked to Brizi [Smoki's cousin, then about 30 years old and working at a Tirana radio station]. He said he knows the place [E për-7-shme]. Described the owner [referring to Hatibi] as 'a Muslim poet. A cool guy. Known for writing lyrics, songs, in the 1990s. Then he went into faith. Now he has this kafe-librari. It doesn't look like anything from outside. The opening is small. But inside, it opens up—an interior space for music, reading, studying. It's cool.'"

4. Interview conducted in Tirana, July 22, 2015.

5. Interview conducted in Tirana, June 18, 2018.

6. Initial interview conducted in Tirana, July 15, 2015. Followed up in Tirana, July 26, 2021.

7. When I asked them individually about their reading practices, Arlind and Ataol often replied with expressions such as "We read" or "We kept reading."

8. I interview conducted in Tirana, July 23, 2021.

9. In an interview titled "The End: 'Distant Star,'" Mónica Maristain poses the question, "What's the difference between an authoress and a writer?" Bolaño replies, "Silvina Ocampo is a writer. Marcela Serrano is an authoress. A distance of light years separates them" (Bolaño 2011b, 256).

10. Lloha not only spoke Polish; she also worked as a professional translator in Poland.

11. To date, their collaboration has yielded translations of *A Guide to Philosophy in Six Hours and Fifteen Minutes* (2012), *Ferdydurke* (2014), and *Diary* (2019).

12. My assertion here (about my interlocutors' understanding of the ethics and politics of representation) is based on conversations we had together about the main argument of Johannes Fabian's ([1983] 2014) *Time and the Other: How Anthropology Makes Its Object*. Fabian's critique of anthropology in that work hinged on the fundamental (he called it shizogenic) contradiction between ethnographic research (which was by definition intersubjective, requiring shared time and mutual recognition of coevalness) and anthropological writing (which was shot through with unequal power relations). But Arlind and Ataol did something with Fabian's argument I didn't expect. They turned it on its head, raising the question for me: What happens when it's not the unreflective anthropologist but the fully knowing subjects of ethnography who introduce the distancing devices? When Arlind and Ataol prefaced their remarks to me with caveats such as "in Albania," "in a place like this," "in a small/poor/violent country," or "in the Balkans" they undoubtedly spoke to me through the shared time of ethnographic research, but what they seemed to be saying was, "You can't really understand this, because you don't live here."

13. Interview conducted in Tirana, July 17, 2015.

14. For ethnographic accounts of the broader structure of feeling that Arlind's statement expresses, see Sarah Green's *Notes from the Balkans* (2005) and Dimitris Dalakoglou's (2010) article, "Migrating-Remitting-'Building'-Dwelling."

15. For a recent ethnographic account of the events and reverberations of 1997, see Musaraj (2020).
16. Interview conducted in Tirana, July 22, 2015.
17. As the following investment climate statement reported, "Albanian law protects copyrights . . . [but] regulators are ineffective at collecting fines and prosecutors rarely press charges for IP theft" (U.S. Department of State 2014).
18. Keep in mind, there are some eighty-five more stories like this. The correspondence behind obtaining the rights to publish *Testaments Betrayed*, related in Chapter 2, being another.
19. Though the Albanian currency floats, the general shorthand people use is to move the decimal point two places—making 200 Lekë roughly equivalent to $2.00.
20. In an interview with Minh-ha, Nancy Chen characterized speaking nearby as a technique to "make visible the invisible" (Chen 1992, 86). Minh-ha affirms this interpretation, adding that it is "a speaking that does not objectify. . . . A speaking that reflects on itself and can come very close to a subject without, however, seizing or claiming it" (Chen 1992, 87).
21. The names that came up most when I asked about foreign authors from this period included Remarque, Hemingway, Dreiser, Dostoevsky, Tolstoy, and Dickens. Exceptions to the general rule of state-controlled literature included smuggled books and locally produced illicit literature (Kerbizi 2017, 316).
22. Interview conducted in Kamëz, July 20, 2017.
23. Interview conducted in Kamëz, June 28, 2019.
24. In the passage I was referring to, Kundera wrote, "[Fielding] tries to define the art—that is to determine its raison d'être, to outline the realm of reality it should illuminate, explore, grasp: 'the provision, then, which we have made is no other than *Human Nature.*' . . . In *Tom Jones*, Fielding suddenly interrupts himself in mid-narration to declare that he is dumbfounded by one of the characters, whose behavior the writer finds 'the most unaccountable of all the absurdities which ever entered into the brain of that strange prodigious creature man'; in fact, astonishment at the 'inexplicable' in 'that strange . . . creature man' is for Fielding the prime incitement to writing the novel, the reason for *inventing* it" (2006, 6–7).
25. The specific episode Arlind referred to was from Book I, Chapter XXXIII—Where the novella of the "Ill-Advised Curiosity" is related.
26. Interview conducted in Tirana, July 22, 2015.
27. Readers of Michael Ende's (1983) *The Neverending Story* will recognize this phrase.

CHAPTER 5

Epigraph. The Albanian idiom *E ka jeta* (like the English, So it goes) resists literal translation but means something like, "These are things that happen in one's life" or "This is how life is" (Ataol Kaso 2019, pers. comm., February 41).
1. For anthropological and ethnographic approaches to value and valuation in socialist and postsocialist contexts, see Archer (2018), Berdahl, Bunzl, and Lampland (2000), Burawoy and Verdery (1999), Fehérváry (2013), Ghodsee (2011), Mandel and Humphrey (2002), Musaraj (2020), and Verdery (2003).
2. Unless otherwise noted, the direct speech quoted in this chapter comes from the narration I recorded with Ataol in his Tirana office on June 20, 2016.

3. See also Margo Rejmer's (2021) *Mud Sweeter than Honey: Voices of Communist Albania*, which addresses relevant themes using a similar, though more literary approach to oral history.

4. For an analysis of the broader corruption discourse in Albania, see Costello, Traficanti, and Bogdani (2014), Elbasani (2017), Jusufi (2018), and Kajsiu (2015).

5. For examples of what I mean, see Biehl (2005), Fassin, Marcis, and Lethata (2008), Fortun (2001), Petryna (2002), and Scheper-Hughes (1992).

6. Ataol Kaso 2019, pers. comm., January 15.

7. On moral economies, see Thompson (1971; 1991), Fassin (2009), and Palomera and Vetta (2016).

8. On revival of faith in formerly atheist Albania, see Montgomery (2019), Doja (2019), and Trix (1994).

9. For further discussion of this phenomenon in postsocialist Albania, see Musaraj (2020); for analysis of related patterns in postsocialist Europe, see Archer (2018), Bodnár and Böröcz (1998), Fehérváry (2013), Harris (2013), and Tsenkova (2009).

10. Interview conducted in Prishtina, June 10, 2016.

11. For a discussion of the epistemological foundations of intersubjective communication, see Fabian, Jarvie, and Kloos (1971); for a nuanced elaboration of the sorts of paradox it can entail, see West (2007).

12. Interview conducted in Tirana, July 4, 2018.

13. Interview conducted in Tirana, June 30, 2017.

CONCLUSION

1. Interview conducted via WhatsApp, June 19, 2020.

2. From an actor-network-theory perspective, I suppose, "what the virus gets from banal droplets from coughing going from one mouth to another" (Latour 2020) should now be added—along with paper, glue, ink, and words—to the list of nonhuman agencies transforming this account.

3. Arlind here was referring to the business Libra të vjetër dhe të përdorur—Old and Used Books (LVP)—that Orges and Eligers started in 2013, using smart phones and social media to contact buyers and a local courier service to handle deliveries and transactions, which are all in cash.

4. The now completed demolition of the National Theatre started before dawn on May 17, 2020—while a group of peaceful activists were still inside hoping to prevent this eventuality. As reported in local media, the scene played out like an object lesson in the forms of violence and corruption that have touched the lives of Tirana residents for many years now. While there is not space here for a detailed account, for a picture of the demolition from a local perspective I quote Alice Taylor, reporting for *Exit News*: "There were tears, outpourings of grief and despair, and utter disbelief as demolition vehicles continued to tear down the walls of one of Tirana's few remaining historic buildings" (Taylor 2021).

5. Here I am reminded of why it's good to keep listening to Fabian (2014) about the uses of time in anthropology: Between the time of recording the fieldnote and writing the account, Arlind upgraded the internet at home.

6. Ataol Kaso 2021, pers. comm., January 8.

7. Ataol Kaso 2021, pers. comm., February 7.

8. I use the term "urban now," which accumulates and preserves traces of the past in the present, in the specific sense Jennifer Robinson proposed, drawing from Walter Benjamin's (1999) analysis of urban modernity, as an analytic category for theorizing "a more global urban studies" (Robinson 2013, 659).

9. See Latour (2005, 5, 46, 129).

10. Interview conducted via WhatsApp, May 15, 2021.

References

Abrahams, Fred. 2015. *Modern Albania: From Dictatorship to Democracy in Europe*. New York: New York University Press.

Abu-Lughod, Lila. 1991. "Writing against Culture." In *Recapturing Anthropology: Working in the Present*, edited by Richard Fox, 137–62. Santa Fe, NM: School of American Research Press.

———. 1997. "The Interpretation of Culture(s) after Television." *Representations*, no. 59 (July): 109–34.

Aliaj, Besnik. 2003. "Albania: A Short History of Housing and Urban Development Models during 1945–1999." Paper presented at the International Conference of the European Network of Housing Research (ENHR), Making Cities Work!, Tirana, 26–28 May.

Aliaj, Besnik, Keida Lulo, and Genc Myftiu. 2003. *Tirana: The Challenge of Urban Development*. Tirana: Cetis.

Anderson, Benedict. 1991. *Imagined Communities: Reflections on the Origin and Spread of Nationalism*. London: Verso.

Appadurai, Arjun. 1986a. "Introduction: Commodities and the Politics of Value." In *The Social Life of Things: Commodities in Cultural Perspective*, edited by Arjun Appadurai, 3–63. Cambridge: Cambridge University Press.

———, ed. 1986b. *The Social Life of Things: Commodities in Cultural Perspective*. Cambridge: Cambridge University Press.

Archer, Rory. 2018. "The Moral Economy of Home Construction in Late Socialist Yugoslavia." *History and Anthropology* 29, no. 2: 141–62.

Ardèvol, Elisenda, Antoni Roig, Gemma San Cornelio, Ruth Pagès, and Pau Alsina. 2010. "Playful Practices: Theorising 'New Media' Cultural Production." In *Theorising Media and Practice*, edited by Birgit Bräuchler and John Postill, 259–79. New York: Berghahn Books.

Arendt, Hannah. 1970. *On Violence*. New York: Harcourt, Brace and World.

Augé, Marc. 2013. *No Fixed Abode: Ethnofiction*. Translated by Chris Turner. New York: Seagull Books.

Baczynska, Gabriela. 2020. "EU Moves to Start Membership Talks with Albania, North Macedonia." *Reuters*, March 23, 2020. https://www.reuters.com/article/us-eu-balkans-idUSKBN21A1AA.

Bakhtin, M. M. 1981. *The Dialogic Imagination: Four Essays*. Translated by Michael Holquist and Caryl Emerson. Austin: University of Texas Press.

Basso, Keith H. 1996. *Wisdom Sits in Places: Landscape and Language among the Western Apache*. Albuquerque: University of New Mexico Press.

Bauman, Zygmunt. 1989. *Modernity and the Holocaust*. Cambridge, UK: Polity Press.

———. 2000. *Liquid Modernity*. Cambridge, UK: Polity Press.

Bedalli, Elona. 2013. "Kaosi Me Biznesin e Librit." *Revista Monitor*, November 23, 2013. https://www.monitor.al/kaosi-me-biznesin-e-librit.

Behar, Ruth. 1993. *Translated Woman: Crossing the Border with Esperanza's Story*. Boston: Beacon Press.

Behar, Ruth, and Deborah A. Gordon, eds. 1995. *Women Writing Culture*. Berkeley: University of California Press.

Benjamin, Walter. 1979. *One Way Street and Other Writings*. Translated by Edmond Jephcott. London: New Left Books.

———. 1999. *The Arcades Project*. Translated by Howard Eiland and Kevin McLaughlin. Cambridge, MA: Harvard University Press.

Berdahl, Daphne, Matti Bunzl, and Martha Lampland, eds. 2000. *Altering States: Ethnographies of Transition in Eastern Europe and the Former Soviet Union*. Ann Arbor: University of Michigan Press.

Biehl, João. 2005. *Vita: Life in a Zone of Social Abandonment*. Berkeley: University of California Press.

Bird, S. Elizabeth. 2010. "From Fan Practice to Mediated Moments: The Value of Practice Theory in the Understanding of Media Audiences." In *Theorising Media and Practice*, edited by Birgit Bräuchler and John Postill, 85–104. New York: Berghahn Books.

Blair, Ann. 2010. *Too Much to Know: Managing Scholarly Information before the Modern Age*. New Haven, CT: Yale University Press.

Bloch, Maurice. 1977. "The Past and the Present in the Present." *Man* 12, no. 2: 278–92.

Bodnár, Judit, and József Böröcz. 1998. "Housing Advantages for the Better Connected? Institutional Segmentation, Settlement Type and Social Network Effects in Hungary's Late State-Socialist Housing Inequalities." *Social Forces* 76, no. 4: 1275–304.

Bolaño, Roberto. 2004. *Distant Star*. Translated by Chris Andrews. New York: New Directions.

———. 2011a. "About *The Savage Detectives*." In *Between Parentheses: Essays, Articles, and Speeches, 1998–2003*, edited by Ignacio Echevarría, translated by Natasha Wimmer, 352–53. New York: New Directions.

———. 2011b. "The End: 'Distant Star' (Interview with Mónica Maristain)." In *Between Parentheses: Essays, Articles, and Speeches, 1998–2003*, edited by Ignacio Echevarría, translated by Natasha Wimmer, 354–70. New York: New Directions.

———. 2011c. "The Vagaries of the Literature of Doom." Translated by Natasha Wimmer. *Hudson Review* 64, no. 1: 95–101.

Bon, Nataša Gregorič. 2019. "Neither the Balkans nor Europe: The 'Where' and 'When' in Present-Day Albania." In *Everyday Life in the Balkans*, edited by David W. Montgomery, 201–10. Bloomington: Indiana University Press.

Borges, Jorge Luis. 1999. *Collected Fictions*. Translated by Andrew Hurley. New York: Penguin Books.

Bourdieu, Pierre. 1977. *Outline of a Theory of Practice*. Cambridge: Cambridge University Press.

———. 1993. "The Field of Cultural Production, or, The Economic World Reversed." In *The Field of Cultural Production: Essays on Art and Literature*, edited by Randal Johnson, 29–73. Cambridge, UK: Polity Press.

Boyarin, Jonathan, ed. 1993a. *The Ethnography of Reading*. Berkeley: University of California Press.

———. 1993b. "Voices around the Text: The Ethnography of Reading at Mesivta Tifereth Jerusalem." In *The Ethnography of Reading*, edited by Jonathan Boyarin, 212–37. Berkeley: University of California Press.

Bräuchler, Birgit, and John Postill, eds. 2010. *Theorising Media and Practice*. New York: Berghahn Books.

Breckenridge, Carol A., ed. 1995. *Consuming Modernity: Public Culture in a South Asian World*. Minneapolis: University of Minnesota Press.

Buda, Aleks, and Xhevat Lloshi. 1985. *Fjalor enciklopedik shqiptar*. Tiranë: Akademia e Shkencave e RPSSH.

Burawoy, Michael, and Katherine Verdery, eds. 1999. *Uncertain Transition: Ethnographies of Change in the Postsocialist World*. Lanham, MD: Rowman and Littlefield.

Burgen, Stephen. 2018. "'Build It and They Will Come': Tirana's Plan for a 'Kaleidoscope Metropolis.'" *Guardian*, October 29, 2018. http://www.theguardian.com/cities/2018/oct/29/tirana-2030-albania-capital-plan-erion-veliaj.

Campkin, Ben, and Ger Duijzings, eds. 2016. *Engaged Urbanism: Cities and Methodologies*. London: I. B. Tauris.

Casanova, Pascale. 2004. *The World Republic of Letters*. Convergences. Cambridge, MA: Harvard University Press.

Certeau, Michel de. 1988a. "Reading as Poaching." In *The Practice of Everyday Life*, translated by Steven Rendall, 165–76. Berkeley: University of California Press.

———. 1988b. "Walking in the City." In *The Practice of Everyday Life*, translated by Steven Rendall, 91–110. Berkeley: University of California Press.

Chartier, Roger. 1994. *The Order of Books: Readers, Authors, and Libraries in Europe between the Fourteenth and Eighteenth Centuries*. Redwood City, CA: Stanford University Press.

Chawla, Devika. 2014. *Home, Uprooted: Oral Histories of India's Partition*. New York: Fordham University Press.

Chen, Nancy N. 1992. "'Speaking Nearby': A Conversation with Trinh T. Minh-Ha." *Visual Anthropology Review* 8, no. 1: 82–91.

Clifford, James, and George E. Marcus, eds. 1986. *Writing Culture: The Poetics and Politics of Ethnography*. Berkeley: University of California Press.

Cohen, Marilyn, ed. 2013. *Novel Approaches to Anthropology: Contributions to Literary Anthropology*. Lanham, MD: Lexington Books.

Cochran-Smith, Marilyn. 1984. *The Making of a Reader*. New York: Ablex Publishing Corporation.

Costello, Charles, Joseph Traficanti, and Mirela Bogdani. 2014. *Albania Rule of Law Assessment: Final Report*. Bethesda, MD: Democracy International and USAID. http://pdf.usaid.gov/pdf_docs/PA00KHDW.pdf.

Couldry, Nick. 2010. "Theorising Media as Practice." In *Theorising Media and Practice*, edited by Birgit Bräuchler and John Postill, 35–54. New York: Berghahn Books.

Crapanzano, Vincent. 1980. *Tuhami: Portrait of a Moroccan*. Chicago: University of Chicago Press.

Dalakoglou, Dimitris. 2010. "Migrating-Remitting-'Building'-Dwelling: House-Making as 'Proxy' Presence in Postsocialist Albania." *Journal of the Royal Anthropological Institute* 16, no. 4: 761–77.

Darnton, Robert. 1982. "What Is the History of Books?" *Daedalus* 111, no. 3: 65–83.

De Angelis, Rose, ed. 2002. *Between Anthropology and Literature: Interdisciplinary Discourse.* London: Routledge.

Dervish, Kastriot. 2016. *Lëvizja Komuniste Në Vitet 1924–1944 Dhe Formimi i PKSH-Së.* Tiranë: Shtëpia Botuese 55.

De Waal, Clarissa. 2014. *Albania: Portrait of a Country in Transition.* London: I. B. Tauris.

Doja, Albert. 2019. "The Everyday of Religion and Politics in the Balkans." In *Everyday Life in the Balkans,* edited by David W. Montgomery, 321–35. Bloomington: Indiana University Press.

Duclos, Diane. 2019. "When Ethnography Does Not Rhyme with Anonymity: Reflections on Name Disclosure, Self-Censorship and Storytelling." *Ethnography* 20, no. 2: 175–83.

Duijzings, Ger. 2002. "Religion and the Politics of 'Albanianism': Naim Frashëri's Bektashi Writings." In *Albanian Identities: Myth and History,* edited by Stephanie Schwandner-Sievers and Bernd Jürgen Fischer, 60–69. Bloomington: Indiana University Press.

———. 2011. "Dictators, Dogs, and Survival in a Post-Totalitarian City." In *Urban Constellations,* edited by Matthew Gandy, 145–48. Berlin: Jovis.

———. 2018. "Engaged Urbanism: Situated and Experimental Methodologies for Fairer Cities." Paper presented at the Laboratorit të Antropologjisë Urbane pranë Institutit të Antropologjisë Kulturore dhe Studimit të Artit, Tiranë, June 12, 2018.

Dulin, Ken L. 1974. "The Sociology of Reading." *Journal of Educational Research* 67, no. 9: 392–96.

Eisenstein, Elizabeth L. 1983. *The Printing Revolution in Early Modern Europe.* Cambridge: Cambridge University Press.

Elbasani, Arolda. 2017. "Judiciary as a Mechanism of State Capture: External Actors, Party Patronage and Informality." *Perspectives: Political Analyses and Commentary,* no. 3: 26–30.

Elsie, Robert. 1995. *History of Albanian Literature.* 2 vols. New York: Columbia University Press.

———. 2005. *Albanian Literature: A Short History.* London: I. B. Tauris.

Ende, Michael. 1983. *The Neverending Story.* Translated by Ralph Manheim. New York: Penguin Books.

Fabian, Johannes. 1993. "Keep Listening: Ethnography and Reading." In *The Ethnography of Reading,* edited by Jonathan Boyarin, 80–97. Berkeley: University of California Press.

———. (1983) 2014. *Time and the Other: How Anthropology Makes Its Object.* New York: Columbia University Press.

Fabian, Johannes, I. C. Jarvie, and Peter Kloos. 1971. "On Professional Ethics and Epistemological Foundations." *Current Anthropology* 12, no. 2: 230–32.

Fassin, Didier. 2009. "Moral Economies Revisited." *Annales: Histoire, Sciences Sociales* 64, no. 6: 1237–66.

———. 2014. "True Life, Real Lives." *American Ethnologist* 41, no. 1: 40–55.

Fassin, Didier, Frédéric Le Marcis, and Todd Lethata. 2008. "Life and Times of Magda A: Telling a Story of Violence in South Africa." *Current Anthropology* 49, no. 2: 225–46.

Febvre, Lucien Paul Victor, and Henri-Jean Martin. 1976. *The Coming of the Book: The Impact of Printing 1450–1800*. London: N. L. B.

Fehérváry, Krisztina. 2013. *Politics in Color and Concrete: Socialist Materialities and the Middle Class in Hungary*. Bloomington: Indiana University Press.

Feld, Steven. 1987. "Dialogic Editing: Interpreting How Kaluli Read Sound and Sentiment." *Cultural Anthropology* 2, no. 2: 190–210.

Fortun, Kim. 2001. *Advocacy after Bhopal: Environmentalism, Disaster, New Global Orders*. Chicago: University of Chicago Press.

Fournier, Laurent Sébastien, and Jean-Marie Privat. 2016. "The Anthropology of Literature in France: Birth and Becoming of a New Field of Studies." *Anthropological Journal of European Cultures* 25, no. 1: 81–95.

Frashëri, Sami. 1899. *Shqipëria ç'ka Qënë, ç'është e ç'do Të Bëhet*. Bucharest: Shoqëria Dituria.

———. 2013. "Albania, What It Was, What It Is and What It Will Be?" In *National Romanticism: The Formation of National Movements*, edited by Balázs Trencsényi and Michal Kopeček, translated by Rigels Halili, 297–304. Discourses of Collective Identity in Central and Southeast Europe 1770–1945, vol. 2. Budapest: Central European University Press.

———. 2019. "Shqipëria - Ç'ka Qënë, ç'është e ç'do Të Bëhetë? Mendime Për Shpëtimt Të Mëmëdheut Nga Reziket Që e Kanë Rethuarë." In *Texts and Documents of Albanian History*, translated by Robert Elsie. http://www.albanianhistory.net/1899_Frasheri/index.html.

Geertz, Clifford. 1973a. *The Interpretation of Cultures: Selected Essays*. New York: Basic Books.

———. 1973b. "Thick Description: Toward an Interpretive Theory of Culture." In *The Interpretation of Cultures: Selected Essays*, 1–30. Boston: Basic Books.

———. 1988. *Works and Lives: The Anthropologist as Author*. Redwood City, CA: Stanford University Press.

Gharraie, Jonathan. 2011. "Why We Read 'Don Quixote.'" *Paris Review*, March 28, 2011. www.theparisreview.org/blog/2011/03/28/why-we-read-don-quixote.

Ghodsee, Kristen. 2011. *Lost in Transition: Ethnographies of Everyday Life after Communism*. Durham, NC: Duke University Press.

Ginsburg, Faye D. 1995. "Mediating Culture: Indigenous Media, Ethnographic Film, and the Production of Identity." In *Fields of Vision: Essays in Film Studies, Visual Anthropology, and Photography*, edited by Leslie Devereaux and Roger Hillman, 256–91. Berkeley: University of California Press.

Ginsburg, Faye D., Lila Abu-Lughod, and Brian Larkin, eds. 2002. *Media Worlds: Anthropology on New Terrain*. Berkeley: University of California Press.

Ginzburg, Carlo. 1992. *The Cheese and the Worms: The Cosmos of a Sixteenth-Century Miller*. Baltimore, MD: Johns Hopkins University Press.

Girard, René. 1966. *Deceit, Desire, and the Novel: Self and Other in Literary Structure*. Translated by Yvonne Freccero. Baltimore, MD: Johns Hopkins University Press.

Gjevor, Elis. 2019. "How One Theatre Tells the Unfolding Story of Albania's Political Crisis." *TRT World*, April 17, 2019. https://www.trtworld.com/magazine/how-one-theatre-tells-the-unfolding-story-of-albania-s-political-crisis-25939.

Gombrowicz, Witold. 2000. *Ferdydurke*. Translated by Danuta Borchardt. New Haven, CT: Yale University Press.

———. 2014. *Ferdydurke*. Translated by Edlira Lloha. Tiranë: Pika pa sipërfaqe.

Goody, Jack. 1968a. Introduction to *Literacy in Traditional Societies*, edited by Jack Goody, 1–26. Cambridge: Cambridge University Press.

———, ed. 1968b. *Literacy in Traditional Societies*. Cambridge: Cambridge University Press.

Grant, Tina, ed. 2004. "Amazon.Com, Inc." In *International Directory of Company Histories*, no. 56: 12–15. Detroit, MI: St. James Press.

Green, Sarah F. 2005. *Notes from the Balkans: Locating Marginality and Ambiguity on the Greek-Albanian Border*. Princeton, NJ: Princeton University Press.

Griswold, Wendy. 2000. *Bearing Witness: Readers, Writers, and the Novel in Nigeria*. Princeton Studies in Cultural Sociology. Princeton, NJ: Princeton University Press.

Gupta, Akhil, and James Ferguson, eds. 1997. *Anthropological Locations: The Boundaries and Grounds of a Field Science*. Berkeley: University of California Press.

Halili, Rigels. 2013. "Faik Konitza: The Political Crisis in Albania." In *Modernism: The Creation of Nation-States*, edited by Ahmet Ersoy, Maciej Górny, and Vangelis Kechriotis, 175–79. Discourses of Collective Identity in Central and Southeast Europe 1770–1945, vol. 3. Budapest: Central European University Press.

Halvorson, Britt, and Ingie Hovland. 2021. "Reconnecting Language and Materiality in Christian Reading: A Comparative Analysis of Two Groups of Protestant Women." *Comparative Studies in Society and History* 63, no. 2: 499–529.

Handler, Richard, and Daniel Segal. 1990. *Jane Austen and the Fiction of Culture: An Essay on the Narration of Social Realities*. Tucson: University of Arizona Press.

Hannerz, Ulf. 1980. *Exploring the City: Inquiries toward an Urban Anthropology*. New York: Columbia University Press.

Harris, Steven. 2013. *Communism on Tomorrow Street: Mass Housing and Everyday Life after Stalin*. Baltimore, MD: Johns Hopkins University Press.

Hartog, François. 2016. *Regimes of Historicity: Presentism and Experiences of Time*. Translated by Saskia Brown. New York: Columbia University Press.

Hatibi, Ervin. 2019. "Memories of Foreign Love." In *Everyday Life in the Balkans*, edited by David W. Montgomery, 372–83. Bloomington: Indiana University Press.

Hobart, Mark. 1999. "After Anthropology?: A View from Too Near." Unpublished Paper. https://www.academia.edu/42103734/After_Anthropology_a_view_from_too_near.

Hobsbawm, E. J. 1994. *The Age of Extremes: A History of the World, 1914–1991*. New York: Pantheon Books.

Hodges, Matt. 2019. "History's Impasse: Radical Historiography, Leftist Elites, and the Anthropology of Historicism in Southern France." *Current Anthropology* 60, no. 3: 391–413.

Horkheimer, Max, and Theodor W. Adorno. 2002. "The Culture Industry: Enlightenment as Mass Deception." In *Dialectic of Enlightenment: Philosophical Fragments*, edited by Gunzelin Schmid Noerr, translated by Edmund Jephcott. Redwood City, CA: Stanford University Press.

Hornborg, Alf. 2021. "Objects Don't Have Desires: Toward an Anthropology of Technology beyond Anthropomorphism." *American Anthropologist* 123, no. 4: 753–66.

Hoxha, Enver. 1980. "Literature and Art Should Serve to Temper People with Class Consciousness for the Construction of Socialism." In *Selected Works of Enver Hoxha*, III: 832–59. Tirana: Institute of Marxist-Leninist Studies.

———. 1982. *The Titoites*. Tirana: Institute of Marxist-Leninist Studies.

Humphrey, Caroline. 2009. "The Mask and the Face: Imagination and Social Life in Russian Chat Rooms and Beyond." *Ethnos*, no. 1 (March): 31–50.

Hysa, Armanda. 2013. "Albanian Ethnography at the Margins of History, 1947–1991: Documenting the Nation in Historical Materialist Terms." In *The Anthropological Field on the Margins of Europe, 1945–1991*, edited by Aleksandar Boskovic and Chris Hann, 129–51. Münster: LIT Verlag.

INSTAT. 2020a. "Diaspora e Shqipërisë Në Shifra." Tiranë.

———. 2020b "Statistikat e Popullsisë." Tiranë: Republika e Shqipërisë Instituti i Statistikave. http://www.instat.gov.al/al/temat/treguesit-demografik%C3%AB-dhe-social%C3%AB/popullsia.

———. 2021. "Statistikat e Kulturës." Tiranë: Republika e Shqipërisë Instituti i Statistikave. http://www.instat.gov.al/al/temat/treguesit-demografik%C3%AB-dhe-social%C3%AB/kultura.

Iser, Wolfgang. 1978. *The Act of Reading: A Theory of Aesthetic Response*. Baltimore, MD: Johns Hopkins University Press.

———. 1989. "Toward a Literary Anthropology." In *Prospecting: From Reader Response to Literary Anthropology*, 262–84. Baltimore, MD: Johns Hopkins University Press.

Ivins, William Mills. 1953. *Prints and Visual Communication*. Cambridge, MA: Harvard University Press.

Jackson, Michael. 2013a. *The Other Shore: Essays on Writers and Writing*. Berkeley: University of California Press.

———. 2013b. *The Wherewithal of Life: Ethics, Migration, and the Question of Well-Being*. Berkeley: University of California Press.

Jerolmack, Colin, and Alexandra K. Murphy. 2019. "The Ethical Dilemmas and Social Scientific Trade-Offs of Masking in Ethnography." *Sociological Methods and Research* 48, no. 4: 801–27.

Johns, Adrian. 1998. *The Nature of the Book: Print and Knowledge in the Making*. Chicago: University of Chicago Press.

Jusufi, Islam. 2018. "Clientelism and Informality in Albania." *Eastern Journal of European Studies* 9, no. 1: 133–50.

Kajsiu, Blendi. 2015. *A Discourse Analysis of Corruption: Instituting Neoliberalism against Corruption in Albania, 1998–2005*. London: Routledge.

Kalo, Sofia. 2017. "'The Red Kiss of the Past That Does Not Pass': State Socialism in Albanian Visual Art Today." *Visual Anthropology Review* 33, no. 1: 51–61.

Keefe, Eugene K., Sarah Jane Elpern, William Giloane, James M. Moore Jr., Stephen Peters, and Eston T. White. 1971. *Area Handbook for Albania*. Washington, DC: US Government Printing Office.

Kerbizi, Marisa. 2017. "Communist Ideology and Its Impact on Albanian Literature." In *Ideological Messaging and the Role of Political Literature*, edited by Önder Çakırtaş, 200–221. Hershey, PA: IGI Global.

King, Russell, Nicola Mai, and Stephanie Schwandner-Sievers, eds. 2005. *The New Albanian Migration*. Lancaster: Sussex Academic Press.

Kjaerulff, Jens. 2010. "A Barthian Approach to Practice and Media: Internet Engagements among Teleworkers in Rural Denmark." In *Theorising Media and Practice*, edited by Birgit Bräuchler and John Postill, 213–31. New York: Berghahn Books.

Kopytoff, Igor. 1986. "The Cultural Biography of Things: Commoditization as Process." In *The Social Life of Things: Commodities in Cultural Perspective*, edited by Arjun Appadurai, 64–91. Cambridge: Cambridge University Press.

Koselleck, Reinhart. 1985. *Futures Past: On the Semantics of Historical Time*. Translated by Kieth Tribe. Cambridge, MA: MIT Press.

Kosta, Barjaba, and Joniada Kosta. 2015. "Embracing Emigration: The Migration-Development Nexus in Albania." Migration Policy Institute, September 10, 2015. https://www.migrationpolicy.org/article/embracing-emigration-migration-development-nexus-albania.

Kundera, Milan. 1984. "The Tragedy of Central Europe." Translated by Edmund White. *New York Review of Books*, April 26, 1984.

———. 1996. *Testaments Betrayed: An Essay in Nine Parts*. Translated by Linda Asher. New York: Harper Collins.

———. 2006. *The Curtain: An Essay in Seven Parts*. Translated by Linda Asher. New York: Harper Collins.

Kunkel, Benjamin. 2007. "In the Sonora." *London Review of Books*, September 6, 2007. https://www.lrb.co.uk/the-paper/v29/n17/benjamin-kunkel/in-the-sonora.

Kurti, Albin. 2017. "Panairi i 19të i librit." Facebook, June 7, 2017. https://www.facebook.com/albini2017/posts/230556740777551.

Lambek, Michael. 2003. *The Weight of the Past: Living with History in Mahajanga, Madagascar*. New York: Palgrave Macmillan.

Latour, Bruno. 1993. *We Have Never Been Modern*. Translated by Catherine Porter. Cambridge, MA: Harvard University Press.

———. 2005. *Reassembling the Social: An Introduction to Actor-Network-Theory*. New York: Oxford University Press.

———. 2020. "What Protective Measures Can You Think of So We Don't Go Back to the Pre-Crisis Production Model?" *Versopolis Review*, April 24, 2020. https://www.versopolis.com/festival-of-hope/festival-of-hope/846/what-protective-measures-can-you-think-of-so-we-don-t-go-back-to-the-pre-crisis-production-model.

Laurenson, John. 2019. "How a Recent Ban on Gambling in Albania Is Impacting the Country." *Marketplace*, February 18, 2019. https://www.marketplace.org/2019/02/18/how-recent-ban-gambling-albania-impacting-country.

Leach, James. 2009. "Freedom Imagined: Morality and Aesthetics in Open Source Software Design." *Ethnos: Journal of Anthropology* 74, no. 1: 51–71.

Lelaj, Olsi. 2015. *Nën Shenjën e Modernitetit*. Tiranë: Pika pa sipërfaqe.

Levinas, Emmanuel. 1987. *Time and the Other and Additional Essays*. Pittsburgh, PA: Duquesne University Press.

Lévi-Strauss, Claude. 1963. *Totemism*. Translated by Rodney Needham. Boston: Beacon Press.

Lewis, C. S. 1950. *The Literary Impact of the Authorised Version*. London: Athlone Press.

Likmeta, Besar. 2011. "Book Corner Carries Flame For Albania's Lost Poets." *Balkan Insight*, July 12, 2011. https://balkaninsight.com/2011/07/12/book-corner-carries-flame-for-albania-s-lost-poets.

Long, Elizabeth. 1993. "Textual Interpretation as Collective Action." In *The Ethnography of Reading*, edited by Jonathan Boyarin, 180–211. Berkeley: University of California Press.

Low, Setha M., ed. 1999. *Theorizing the City: The New Urban Anthropology Reader*. New Brunswick, NJ: Rutgers University Press.

Lukacs, Gabriella. 2013. "Dreamwork: Cell Phone Novelists, Labor, and Politics in Contemporary Japan." *Cultural Anthropology* 28, no. 1: 44–64.

Mahmood, Saba. 2005. *Politics of Piety: The Islamic Revival and the Feminist Subject*. Princeton, NJ: Princeton University Press.

Malinowski, Bronislaw. 1922. *Argonauts of the Western Pacific*. New York: E. P. Dutton.

Malkki, Liisa. 1997. "News and Culture: Transitory Phenomena and the Fieldwork Tradition." In *Anthropological Locations: The Boundaries and Grounds of a Field Science*, edited by Akhil Gupta and James Ferguson, 86–101. Berkeley: University of California Press.

Mandel, Ruth, and Caroline Humphrey, eds. 2002. *Markets and Moralities: Ethnographies of Postsocialism*. New York: Berg.

Marcus, George E., and Dick Cushman. 1982. "Ethnographies as Texts." *Annual Review of Anthropology*, no. 11: 25.

Martínez, Francisco, ed. 2020. *Politics of Recuperation: Repair and Recovery in Post-Crisis Portugal*. London: Routledge.

Marx, Karl. (1867) 1976. *Capital: Volume 1: A Critique of Political Economy*. Translated by Ben Fowkes. New York: Penguin Classics.

Marx, Karl, and Friedrich Engels. (1848) 1998. *The Communist Manifesto*. London: Verso.

Mauss, Marcel. 1973. "Techniques of the Body." *Economy and Society* 2, no. 1: 70–88.

Mayer, Vicki, Miranda J. Banks, and John Thornton Caldwell, eds. 2009. *Production Studies: Cultural Studies of Media Industries*. New York: Routledge.

McGranahan, Carole, ed. 2020. *Writing Anthropology: Essays on Craft and Commitment*. Durham, NC: Duke University Press.

Mëhilli, Elidor. 2017. *From Stalin to Mao: Albania and the Socialist World*. Ithaca, NY: Cornell University Press.

Metani, Heltor. 2005. "Pjesë e Së Tërës, Me Emrin Livadhja." *Forumi Horizont*, June 8, 2005. http://www.forumihorizont.com.

Miller, Daniel, ed. 2005. "Materiality: An Introduction." In *Materiality*, 1–50. Durham, NC: Duke University Press.

Minh-Ha, Trinh T., dir. 1982. *Reassemblage: From the Firelight to the Screen*. New York: Women Make Movies, 16mm, 40 minutes.

Misha, Piro. 2002. "Invention of a Nationalism: Myth and Amnesia." In *Albanian Identities: Myth and History*, edited by Stephanie Schwandner-Sievers and Bernd Jürgen Fischer, 33–48. Bloomington: Indiana University Press.

Montgomery, David W. 2019. "'The Hardest Time Was the Time without Morality': Religion and Social Navigation in Albania." In *Everyday Life in the Balkans*, edited by David W. Montgomery, 265–77. Bloomington: Indiana University Press.

Morgan, Peter. 2016. "The European Origins of Albania in Ismail Kadare's *The File on H*." In *The Novel and Europe*, edited by Andrew Hammond, 101–13. London: Palgrave Macmillan.

Murati, V. 2016. "Godina Historike e Akademisë Së Shkencave, Shpallet Monument i Kategorisë Së Parë." *Gazeta Mapo*, March 24, 2016. https://gazetamapo.al/godina-historike-e-akademise-se-shkencave-shpallet-monument-i-kategorise-se-pare.

Musaraj, Smoki. 2018. "Corruption, Right On!: Hidden Cameras, Cynical Satire, and Banal Intimacies of Anti-Corruption." *Current Anthropology* 59, suppl. 18: S105–16.

———. 2020. *Tales of Albarado: Ponzi Logics of Accumulation in Postsocialist Albania*. Ithaca, NY: Cornell University Press.

———. 2021. "Temporalities of Concrete: Housing Imaginaries in Albania." In *Remitting, Restoring, and Building Contemporary Albania*, edited by Nataša Gregorič Bon and Smoki Musaraj. Cham, Switzerland: Palgrave Macmillan.

Napolitano, Valentina. 2015. "Anthropology and Traces." *Anthropological Theory* 15, no. 1: 47–67.

Narayan, Kirin. 2007. "Tools to Shape Texts: What Creative Nonfiction Can Offer Ethnography." *Anthropology and Humanism* 32, no. 2: 130–44.

———. 2012. *Alive in the Writing: Crafting Ethnography in the Company of Chekhov*. Chicago: University of Chicago Press.

Nic Craith, Mairead, and Laurent Sebastian Fournier. 2016. "Literary Anthropology: The Sub-Disciplinary Context." In "Literature and Anthropology," ed. Mairead Nic Craith and Laurent Sebastian Fournier. Special issue, *Anthropological Journal of European Cultures* 25, no. 2 (January): 1–8.

Nussbaum, Martha. 1990. *Love's Knowledge: Essays on Philosophy and Literature*. New York: Oxford University Press.

Ortega y Gasset, José. 1959. "The Difficulty of Reading." Translated by Clarence E. Parmenter. *Diogenes* 7, no. 28: 1–17.

Ortner, Sherry B. 1984. "Theory in Anthropology since the Sixties." *Comparative Studies in Society and History* 26, no. 1: 126–66.

———. 2009. "Studying Sideways: Ethnographic Access in Hollywood." In *Production Studies: Cultural Studies of Media Industries*, edited by Vicki Mayer, Miranda J. Banks, and John Thornton Caldwell, 175–89. New York: Routledge.

———. 2013. *Not Hollywood: Independent Film at the Twilight of the American Dream*. Durham, NC: Duke University Press.

———. 2016. "Dark Anthropology and Its Others." *HAU: Journal of Ethnographic Theory* 6, no. 1: 47.

PabloPicasso.org. 2021. "Don Quixote, 1955 by Pablo Picasso." https://www.pablopicasso. org/don-quixote.jsp.

Palomera, Jaime, and Theodora Vetta. 2016. "Moral Economy: Rethinking a Radical Concept." *Anthropological Theory* 16, no. 4: 413–32.

Pandian, Anand. 2014. *Ayya's Accounts: A Ledger of Hope in Modern India.* Bloomington: Indiana University Press.

Pandian, Anand, and Stuart J. McLean, eds. 2017. *Crumpled Paper Boat: Experiments in Ethnographic Writing.* Durham, NC: Duke University Press.

Pardo, Italo, and Giuliana B. Prato, eds. 2016. *Anthropology in the City: Methodology and Theory.* London: Routledge.

———, eds. 2018. *The Palgrave Handbook of Urban Ethnography.* New York: Palgrave Macmillan.

Pedrazzi, Nicola. 2015. "Un caffè e una storia a Tirana." Erodoto108, February 11, 2015. https://www.erodoto108.com/un-caffe-e-una-storia-a-tirana.

Perec, Georges. 2008. "Reading: A Socio-Psychological Outline." In *Species of Spaces and Other Pieces,* translated by John Sturrock, 174–85. New York: Penguin Classics.

Petryna, Adriana. 2002. *Life Exposed: Biological Citizens after Chernobyl.* Princeton, NJ: Princeton University Press.

Pettifer, James. 2013. "Ihsan Bey Toptani, Journalist and Political Activist." *Dielli | The Sun,* June 27, 2013. https://gazetadielli.com/ihsan-bey-toptani-journalist-and-political-activist.

Pipa, Arshi. 1978. *Albanian Literature: Social Perspectives.* München: R. Trofenik.

———. 1991. *Contemporary Albanian Literature.* New York: Columbia University Press.

Powdermaker, Hortense. 1950. *Hollywood, the Dream Factory: An Anthropologist Looks at the Movie-Makers.* Boston: Little, Brown.

Prifti, Peter. 1978. *Socialist Albania Since 1944.* Cambridge, MA: MIT Press.

Proust, Marcel. 2003. *In Search of Lost Time,* vol. I: *Swann's Way.* Edited by D. J. Enright, translated by C. K. Scott-Moncrieff and Terence Kilmartin. New York: Modern Library.

Radway, Janice A. 1991. *Reading the Romance: Women, Patriarchy, and Popular Literature.* Chapel Hill: University of North Carolina Press.

Rakipi, Albert. 2017. "Against Gambling." *Tirana Times,* September 13, 2017. https://www. aiis-albania.org/?q=node/147.

Rapport, Nigel. 1993. *Diverse World-Views in an English Village.* Edinburgh: Edinburgh University Press.

———. 1994. *The Prose and the Passion: Anthropology, Literature, and the Writing of E. M. Forster.* Manchester: Manchester University Press.

———. 2012. "Literary Anthropology." *Oxford Bibliographies,* last modified, January 11, 2012. DOI: 10.1093/obo/9780199766567-0067.

Reed, Adam. 2011. *Literature and Agency in English Fiction Reading: A Study of the Henry Williamson Society.* Toronto: University of Toronto Press.

Rejmer, Margo. 2021. *Mud Sweeter than Honey: Voices of Communist Albania.* Translated by Zosia Krasodomska-Jones and Antonia Lloyd-Jones. New York: Restless Books.

Reyes, Victoria. 2018. "Three Models of Transparency in Ethnographic Research: Naming Places, Naming People, and Sharing Data." *Ethnography* 19, no. 2: 204–26.

Robinson, Jennifer. 2013. "The Urban Now: Theorising Cities beyond the New." *European Journal of Cultural Studies* 16, no. 6: 659–77.

———. 2016. "Thinking Cities through Elsewhere: Comparative Tactics for a More Global Urban Studies." *Progress in Human Geography* 40, no. 1: 3–29.

Rogers, Douglas. 2010. "Postsocialisms Unbound: Connections, Critiques, Comparisons." *Slavic Review* 69, no. 1: 1–15.

Rosaldo, Renato. 1989. *Culture and Truth: The Remaking of Social Analysis.* Boston: Beacon Press.

Rosen, Matthew. 2014. *Accidental Communities: Ordinary Reading and Urban Sociality among Marathi-Speaking Migrants in Pune, India.* New York: The New School.

———. 2015. "Ethnographies of Reading: Beyond Literacy and Books." *Anthropological Quarterly* 88, no. 4: 1059–84.

———. 2018. "Accidental Communities: Chance Operations in Urban Life and Field Research." *Ethnography* 19, no. 3: 312–35.

Rosenberg, Tina. 1994. "Albania: The Habits of the Heart." *World Policy Journal* 11, no. 4: 85.

Rothenbuhler, Eric W., and Mihai Coman, eds. 2005. *Media Anthropology.* Thousand Oaks, CA: Sage.

Rouch, Jean and Edgar Morin, dirs. 1961. *Chronique d'un été.* Paris: Argos-Films, 35mm, 85 minutes.

Rylko-Bauer, Barbara. 2014. *A Polish Doctor in the Nazi Camps: My Mother's Memories of Imprisonment, Immigration, and a Life Remade.* Norman: University of Oklahoma Press.

Saavedra, Miguel De Cervantes. 2011. *Don Quixote.* Translated by Tom Lathrop. New York: Signet.

Sadana, Rashmi. 2012. *English Heart, Hindi Heartland: The Political Life of Literature in India.* Berkeley: University of California Press.

Sarris, Greg. 1993. "Keeping Slug Woman Alive: The Challenge of Reading in a Reservation Classroom." In *The Ethnography of Reading,* edited by Jonathan Boyarin, 238–69. Berkeley: University of California Press.

Sartre, Jean-Paul, and Benny Lévy. 1996. *Hope Now: The 1980 Interviews.* Translated by Adrian van den Hoven. Chicago: University of Chicago Press.

SBSH. 2012. Homepage, Shoqata e Botuesve Shqiptarë, accessed April 24, 2022. https://shbsh.al/wp2.

Schatzki, Theodore R. 1996. *Social Practices: A Wittgensteinian Approach to Human Activity and the Social.* Cambridge: Cambridge University Press.

Scheper-Hughes, Nancy. 1992. *Death without Weeping: The Violence of Everyday Life in Brazil.* Berkeley: University of California Press.

Schulz, Bruno. (1934) 1977. *The Street of Crocodiles.* Translated by Celina Wieniewska. New York: Penguin Books.

Schwandner-Sievers, Stephanie. 2002. "Narratives of Power: Capacities of Myth in Albania." In *Albanian Identities: Myth and History,* edited by Stephanie Schwandner-Sievers and Bernd Jürgen Fischer, 3–30. Bloomington: Indiana University Press.

———. 2004a. "Albanians, Albanianism and the Strategic Subversion of Stereotypes." In *The Balkans and the West: Constructing the European Other, 1945–2003*, edited by Andrew Hammond, 110–26. Aldershot: Ashgate Pub Limited.

———. 2004b. "Times Past: References for the Construction of Local Order in Present-Day Albania." In *Balkan Identities: Nation and Memory*, edited by Maria Todorova, 110–26. London: C. Hurst.

Seiller, Louis. 2017. "Albanie: Ces éditeurs indépendants qui se battent pour la diffusion du livre et de la littérature." Balkonfluences: Sound, Words and Images on South-Eastern Europe, February 12, 2017. https://balkonfluences.net/2017/02/12/albanie-ces-editeurs-independants-qui-se-battent-pour-la-diffusion-du-livre-et-de-la-litterature.

Sennett, Richard. 1969. *Classic Essays on the Culture of Cities*. New York: Appleton-Century-Crofts.

Shehu, Bashkim. 2001. "The Dictator's Library." In *Autodafe: The Journal of the International Parliament of Writers*, no. 2: 185–91.

Sherman, William H. 2008. *Used Books: Marking Readers in Renaissance England*. Philadelphia: University of Pennsylvania Press.

Shipe, Timothy. 2012. "A Bibliographer in the Balkans: A(lbania) to Z(agreb)." *WESS Newsletter* 36, no. 1. https://acrl.ala.org/ess/newsletters/wess-newsletter-archive/wess-newsletter-fall-2012/a-bibliographer-in-the-balkans-a-lbania-to-z-agreb.

Sneath, David, Martin Holbraad, and Morten Axel Pedersen. 2009. "Technologies of the Imagination: An Introduction." *Ethnos: Journal of Anthropology* 74, no. 1: 5–30.

Spitulnik, Debra. 2010. "Thick Context, Deep Epistemology: A Meditation on Wide-Angle Lenses on Media, Knowledge Production, and the Concept of Culture." In *Theorising Media and Practice*, edited by Birgit Bräuchler and John Postill, 105–26. New York: Berghahn Books.

Spradley, James P., and George E. McDonough. 1973. *Anthropology through Literature: Cross-Cultural Perspectives*. Boston: Little, Brown.

Stewart, Charles. 2016. "Historicity and Anthropology." *Annual Review of Anthropology* 45, no. 1: 79–94.

Taylor, Alice Elizabeth. 2021. "Comment: The Demolition of the Albanian National Theatre, One Year On." Exit - Explaining Albania, May 17, 2021. https://exit.al/en/2021/05/17/comment-the-demolition-of-the-albanian-national-theatre-one-year-on.

Taylor, Lucien. 1996. "Iconophobia." *Transition*, no. 69: 64–88.

Thompson, E. P. 1971. "The Moral Economy of the English Crowd in the Eighteenth Century." *Past and Present*, no. 50: 76–136.

———. 1991. *Customs in Common*. New York: New Press.

Tochka, Nicholas. 2016. *Audible States: Socialist Politics and Popular Music in Albania*. New York: Oxford University Press.

Toena. 2013. "Historiku i Shtëpisë Botuese." http://www.toena.com.al.

Transparency International. 2019. "Corruption Perceptions Index (CPI)." https://www.transparency.org/en/cpi/2019.

Travis, Trish. 1999. "Ideas and Commodities: The Image of the Book." MIT Communications Forum. http://web.mit.edu/comm-forum/legacy/papers/travis.html.

Trix, Frances. 1994. "The Resurfacing of Islam in Albania." *East European Quarterly* 28, no. 4: 533–49.

Tsenkova, Sasha. 2009. *Housing Policy Reforms in Postsocialist Europe: Lost in Transition.* Heidelberg: Physica-Verlag.

Uçi, Alfred. 2010. *Filozofia e donkishotizimit.* Tiranë: Akademia e Shkencave.

US Department of State, Bureau of Economic and Business Affairs. 2014. "Investment Climate Statement - Albania." http://www.state.gov/e/eb/rls/othr/ics/2014/228429.htm.

Vasa, Pashko. (1879) 2013. "The Truth on Albania and Albanians." In *Late Enlightenment: Emergence of the "National Idea."* Edited by Balázs Trencsényi and Michal Kopeček, translated by Edward St. John Fairman, 118–24. Discourses of Collective Identity in Central and Southeast Europe 1770–1945, vol. 1. Budapest: Central European University Press.

Veqilharxhi, Naum. 2013. "A Preface to Young Albanian Boys." In *Late Enlightenment: Emergence of the "National Idea."* Edited by Balázs Trencsényi and Michal Kopeček, translated by Rigels Halili, 258–62. Discourses of Collective Identity in Central and Southeast Europe 1770–1945, vol. 1. Budapest: Central European University Press.

Verdery, Katherine. 2003. *The Vanishing Hectare: Property and Value in Postsocialist Transylvania.* Ithaca, NY: Cornell University Press.

Vullnetari, Julie. 2021. "'Can Love Be Transferred'?: Tracing Albania's History of Migration and the Meaning of Remittances." In *Remitting, Building, and Restoring Contemporary Albania,* edited by Nataša Gregorič Bon and Smoki Musaraj. Cham, Switzerland: Palgrave Macmillan.

Walker, Harry, and Iza Kavedžija. 2015. "Values of Happiness." *HAU: Journal of Ethnographic Theory* 5, no. 3: 1–23.

Warner, Michael. 1990. *The Letters of the Republic: Publication and the Public Sphere in Eighteenth-Century America.* Cambridge, MA: Harvard University Press.

Waterston, Alisse. 2014. *My Father's Wars: Migration, Memory, and the Violence of a Century.* New York: Routledge.

———. 2019. "Intimate Ethnography and the Anthropological Imagination: Dialectical Aspects of the Personal and Political in My Father's Wars." *American Ethnologist* 46, no. 1: 7–19.

Waterston, Alisse, and Barbara Rylko-Bauer. 2006. "Out of the Shadows of History and Memory: Personal Family Narratives in Ethnographies of Rediscovery." *American Ethnologist* 33, no. 3: 397–412.

Waterston, Alisse, and Maria D. Vesperi, eds. 2009. *Anthropology off the Shelf: Anthropologists on Writing.* Malden, MA: Blackwell.

West, Harry. 2007. *Ethnographic Sorcery.* Chicago: University of Chicago Press.

Wiles, Ellen. 2015. *Saffron Shadows and Salvaged Scripts: Literary Life in Myanmar under Censorship and in Transition.* New York: Columbia University Press.

———. 2020. "Three Branches of Literary Anthropology: Sources, Styles, Subject Matter." *Ethnography* 21, no. 2: 280–95.

———. 2021. *Live Literature: The Experience and Cultural Value of Literary Performance Events from Salons to Festivals.* Palgrave Studies in Literary Anthropology. Basingstoke: Palgrave Macmillan.

Wilk, Richard R., and Kelly Michelle Askew, eds. 2002. *The Anthropology of Media: A Reader*. Blackwell Readers in Anthropology 3. Malden, MA: Blackwell Publishers.

Williams, Raymond. 1973. *The Country and the City*. New York: Oxford University Press.

Woodcock, Shannon. 2016. *Life Is War: Surviving Dictatorship in Communist Albania*. Bristol: HammerOn Press.

Wulff, Helena, ed. 2016. *The Anthropologist as Writer: Genres and Contexts in the Twenty-First Century*. New York: Berghahn Books.

———. 2017. *Rhythms of Writing: An Anthropology of Irish Literature*. London: Bloomsbury Academic.

Yan, Yuxin, Woo In Shin, Yoong Xin Pang, Yang Meng, Jianchen Lai, Chong You, Haitao Zhao, Edward Lester, Tao Wu, and Cheng Heng Pang. 2020. "The First 75 Days of Novel Coronavirus (SARS-CoV-2) Outbreak: Recent Advances, Prevention, and Treatment." *International Journal of Environmental Research and Public Health* 17, no. 7. DOI: 10.3390/ijerph17072323.

Yanow, Dvora. 2009. "Dear Author, Dear Reader: The Third Hermeneutic in Writing and Reviewing Ethnography." In *Political Ethnography: What Immersion Contributes to the Study of Power*, edited by Edward Schatz and Myron J. Aronoff, 275–302. Chicago: University of Chicago Press.

Zickel, Raymond E., and Walter R. Iwaskiw, eds. 1994. *Albania: A Country Study*, 2nd ed. Washington, DC: Federal Research Division, Library of Congress.

Zinsser, William. 2006. *On Writing Well: The Classic Guide to Writing Nonfiction*, 7th ed. New York: HarperCollins.

Index

Numbers in *italic* refer to figures.

CPSIA information can be obtained
at www.ICGtesting.com
Printed in the USA
LVHW111623030922
727557LV00018B/267